Fearfully and Wonderfully Made

FEARFULLY
and
WONDERFULLY
MADE

*A Compelling Account of a teenager's Illness
and Recovery That Began with One Teacher,
One Rose, and One Journal*

ROBIN LEWIS HAVERKAMP

XULON PRESS

Xulon Press
2301 Lucien Way #415
Maitland, FL 32751
407.339.4217
www.xulonpress.com

Paperback ISBN-13: 978-1-66286-043-0
Ebook ISBN-13: 978-1-66286-044-7

*W*hen I was a Freshman in High School it was clear that something extremely serious was happening to Robin. But in 1977, so very little was known or discussed about mental illness. I came to faith in Christ after graduation, and my life changed significantly. It was only many years later that I found myself wondering: "What is this illness?"

We grew up in a pre-social media era so it was difficult to stay in touch with old friends. But now, after more than forty years, our childhood friend Holli reconnected us. I finally understand what Robin was facing and navigating when we were young teenagers.

I believe reading her story and journal entries will give many people hope, especially those who are facing deep challenges, chronic illness, heartache, grief and loss. What shines through so beautifully in this book is Robin's heart, and how God can take our brokenness and lead us to wholeness if we give our lives to Him. That is a timeless message, and a lesson we often need to keep relearning through many different and challenging seasons of our lives.

Mary Mallon Lederleitner, PhD
Author of *Women in God's Mission: Accepting
the Invitation to Serve and Lead*

To any person who suffers from clinical depression, anxiety, fear, or anything that would keep you from living the life that God desires for you so you may fully embrace the brain that He has given to you.

For you created my inmost being; you knit me together in my mother's womb. I praise you because I am fearfully and wonderfully made; your works are wonderful, I know that full well. My frame was not hidden from you when I was made in the secret place, when I was woven together in the depths of the earth. Your eyes saw my unformed body; all the days ordained for me were written in your book before one of them came to be. Psalm 139: 13-16

Contents

Introduction

I believe this story and journey is an unbelievable one in many ways. As you read it, you will notice it is composed of forty years of journaling and my current reflections and memories that expand upon and complement the journal entries. While one may read this book and find it intriguing and riveting, my hope and deepest desire is to encourage and strengthen anyone in their faith in God from their life stories. Most importantly, my hope is for anyone to believe and receive Jesus Christ as their personal Savior, thereby having a close relationship with Him.

You will read and learn, as the story begins, that I did not know God and, therefore, did not have a relationship with His Son. As you read my story, you will discover I am not merely sharing my opinion but, rather, my true-life experiences of pain, joy, perseverance, and a rich and blessed life because of Jesus Christ. I believe then that you will appreciate and fully embrace the brain that God has given to you, and know that you are fearfully, complexly, and wonderfully made in his image.

CHAPTER 1

Fall in Lancaster, Ohio

She's so young, the nurses said. My doctor told me that you are having things happen to you that people have when they're in their forties. I wasn't sure about anything except sleepless nights and roller-coaster moods that were clearly unlike the typical hormonal changes that fourteen-year-old teenagers have. It wasn't juvenile diabetes, heart disease, or cancer. My issue was a mental and emotional one that took too many dips and threw me off track. I found myself on the ninth-floor psychiatric unit at Riverside Hospital in Columbus, Ohio.

September/Early October 1977

> The season was fall which meant different things to different people. For children, it was time to return to school, growing academically and socially. For others it meant beauty coming from the maple trees bursting in bright colors of red, orange, and yellow. Along with the cool but comfortable temperatures, the sky was vividly blue, which completed a perfect fall scene.

For others in my hometown of Lancaster, Ohio, fall represented the county fair that was the best in the state; I believed that then and still do today! The rides, the 4-H projects, and other local exhibits brought a country feeling that county fairs seem to do. Of course, the tasty food comprised of the classic menu of candy and caramel apples, cotton candy, corn dogs on a stick, and all the other foods that are unhealthy. Still, they are delicious, and because you're at the fair, you must eat them!

Nobody could forget the home-made chicken sandwiches made by the Lancaster Band Boosters or the Italian sausages. Those were popular with my father for he very seldom if ever missed having one of them, but I remember disliking the green peppers and spices that smothered the sausage. With a combination of continuing school, radiant colors, and the county fair, I'm pretty certain that Lancaster owned its own nostalgia that we so enjoyed individually and as a community. So did I, but the beautiful season of fall was vastly unique for me.

It was my first year of high school, and while my friends were complaining about the transition from middle school to high school, mistakes being made on their academic schedules, and some of them saying that algebra was unbearably difficult, I had a very different view about the change. I had a lot of friends, I was a cheerleader, and the best thing for me was singing. I was so thrilled when I had my first audition and made the freshman ensemble. I remember well the choir director saying to me, "I didn't know you could sing that well." Her comment of approval was so validating mainly because in middle school, she was the orchestra director, and I respected her back then.

Reflecting back to that summer morning, I recall my father asking me, "The school counselor is on the phone and wants to know if you want to take orchestra or choir?" He awakened me from a nice summer's sleep, and I had to make a quick decision. Anxious and excited at the same time, I made the decision and said, "Choir!" I Wondered what my parents would think, especially my mother, for she wasn't there at the time when the counselor called.

It was a tough decision one I struggled to make because I liked playing the violin, and taking private lessons at the United Methodist Church, and then having my recital—all of which I was proud. Still, singing was my "first love," for I began when I was eight years old singing in the privacy of my bedroom to Donny Osmond's "Go Away Little Girl," and songs from David Cassidy's Partridge Family album. Later, I got really brave and in the sixth grade sang in front of a couple of my friends who were twins and the same age as me. We were at a park near my house on Spring Street, and in the middle of the solo, they whispered something to one another. After I finished, they clapped, which made me feel good and honored, that they would listen to someone singing under a tree at the park!

All those sweet memories gave me a confidence in a talent that I thought I had but later, so often doubted. Still, I never stopped singing. It was settled. I signed up for choir in my freshman year at Lancaster High School where many opportunities awaited.

While my peers were living their lives below the sky, I felt like I was soaring off the ground into the sky, like a kite. I was loving everything, including my friends from General Sherman Junior High school and Thomas Ewing Junior High School. There were two junior high schools, and they were located on opposite sides of the town. Cheerleading, singing, and anything else in life, I simply just liked.

One thing I do remember, however, is that my friends were not acting or feeling like that. Then everything changed when I started doing poorly in Earth Science class, barely passing, which meant one thing to me; suspension from the cheerleading squad (we called it squad back then) because I needed to maintain a C average in order to be a cheerleader.

What began as worry and anxiety slowly and eventually turned into restless nights, sadness, and fear, and those nights became sleepless ones. My concentration was impaired, and as a fourteen-year-old, I had absolutely no idea what was happening to me physically, mentally, or emotionally. The euphoria just weeks prior evolved into a very serious mental fog and an unusual sadness.

Chapter 2

Unhealthy and Bizarre Moments

Events Leading Up to October 10, 1977

School resumed after Labor Day, and I was in study hall, the last period of the day. It was very warm in the room, and I began having troubles breathing, so I was gasping for air. This happened a couple of times. I told my mother that I couldn't breathe very well, and the school nurse later said that I was hyperventilating. I'm pretty certain that I was beginning to have troubles in Earth Science then but not yet losing sleep.

Soon I began having sleep deprivation, and my mood was changing from positivity to sadness and worry. The day of school pictures was a very memorable one, in which the photos were taken in the auditorium. The photographer had us come up on the stage, and then he would take the pictures. While I was getting mine taken, and afterward, I thought that my peers were laughing at me. I didn't actually see people laughing. It was not a hallucination, but a delusion, and it was at this time that I began having sleepless nights. The events that occurred beginning October 7, on Friday evening, are the ones I vividly remember. The following things that happened began a very dark time in my life that would change and shape me in ways I could never have imagined.

October 7:

I went to Lancaster High School's homecoming game with my friends. I was with my best friend, Kelli. At this time, I was sick, meaning I hadn't slept for several days. I was acting peculiar, but of course, I didn't know that at the time. I just remember feeling really strange and unusually hyper. Some of my friends were watching the game and paying attention, but most of us were just goofing off and having fun. I didn't understand a lot of the game of football, even though I was a cheerleader!

Consequently, I wasn't cheering that night because back in the late seventies, Lancaster High School comprised of three grades: 10–12. Stanberry Freshman School was where the ninth graders attended, and the freshmen football team wasn't playing football that night.

The game ended, and Kelli's parents took me home. Kelli actually told me in 2017, forty years later that she remembered me laughing a lot when we got in the car, but nothing was funny. She said that she later felt badly because she was frustrated or angry with me. She was annoyed, and who wouldn't be! But she felt so badly because the weekend passed without seeing me, and on Monday morning, I wasn't at school. She told me that all she knew was that her best friend was gone. When you're fourteen, how can you understand anything like this? Teenagers can't even understand themselves with all of the hormonal changes, much less grasp something that I experienced.

I got home, said good night to my parents, and went to bed. It was about 10:00, and I couldn't sleep. I began believing that

I was going to go to Hollywood to be a singer. Johnny Carson was going to interview me. I actually thought he was in my bedroom closet! Again, I was having delusions, not hallucinations. It was more like a fantasy, and I was out of touch with reality. That same evening, I had the radio on, and I remember hearing that the computer would soon be used in the classroom. Now, that was reality! I had another sleepless night.

October 8:

We had a football game, and my dad took me to the bus stop to ride with the football players, coaches, and cheerleaders. It was raining and dark. I knew I was going to the game, but I felt really weird, but again, I wasn't aware and had no clue that something was wrong with me emotionally and mentally.

I had the usual cheerleading uniform on with black-and-white saddle shoes because that's what the cheerleaders wore at Stanberry. We got to the game, and my behavior was strange in that I got mixed up on the cheers and felt very different than anyone. I bought a cup of hot chocolate during half time because it was cold, which was typical weather for football season. Later, my parents thought someone had put a drug in my hot chocolate to make me act so crazy. The game ended; we lost. Everyone got on the bus, and one of the coaches said, "We know what happened." I thought he was talking about me because I acted peculiar during the game, but he was telling the football players where the team went wrong in their plays and overall performance.

We got back from the game, the bus stopped, and the players walked off, followed by the assistant coach, head coach and cheerleaders, but I remained in my seat. I don't recall how the bus driver addressed this issue, but I know she had troubles getting me to leave. She was our neighbor and friend and whose son was in my class and played football that day.

In my world, I was going to Hollywood to be a singer in musical theater. She called my parents after several attempts to get me off the bus. Today, I can still see her looking in her mirror at me, wondering why I stayed in my seat. It was still raining, and Mom came to the door of the bus and was carrying her umbrella. She said, "Come on, Robin; let's go home." I resisted and I still remember her using the umbrella that was half open and half closed. It was a dismal day, perfect for the situation! She was confused, frustrated, and baffled as to why I wouldn't get off the bus. She was impatient and maybe angry or just worried.

I finally went with her, and we went home. It was early afternoon when we got home, and my brother, Jimmy was home from college, but I don't recall where Janice, my sister, was. What I definitely remember is that I sat on the couch, and my parents began asking me if anyone put anything in my hot chocolate. They thought someone had drugged me. Then my brother shook me a little bit to see if I would snap out of this very abnormal behavior. I do know this and appreciate it in an entirely different way today than I ever did.

My brother was twenty years old; my sister was seventeen, so young to see their fourteen-year-old little sister acting, feeling, and behaving in such a way that was crazy, scary, and baffling. Who could comprehend this? My mother, being a registered nurse and a worried mother, called the hospital after figuring that neither she nor anyone else could fix this or get me to think clearly and get me back into reality.

So, we drove to the hospital where Jean, the registered nurse on duty, met with me. A friend of my mother's and of the family, she pleasantly said, "Hi Robin." My mother explained the situation to her ahead of time when she called the hospital, so she knew the basic story. But I didn't recognize her, which must have really scared my mother, confirming her fear that I was emotionally and mentally troubled. After she said hi, she had me lie down on a table and then asked some questions. Then a doctor came in and asked me some general questions about the summer. He commented on my suntan and asked if I had a nice summer.

My friends and I swam every day at the pool in the summer. There were a group of us who played keep away with the tennis ball, and it was so fun, but my friend Kelli and I were the closest. We rode our bikes out to the pool every day and stayed until about 5:00. After the doctor completed what was like a mini physical, he told my mother that Lancaster's hospital couldn't manage this kind of situation and referred us to a mental health clinic in Columbus, which was forty-five minutes north of Lancaster.

By this time, it was midafternoon, and my parents drove to Columbus, and I initially met with a caseworker, and then later, with the doctor on call. While waiting for the doctor to talk with me, at some point I was singing in the halls the song, "You'll Never Walk Alone." The acoustics were incredibly good! There is a very interesting irony. I wasn't walking alone. I had my parents and my siblings who were walking with me, and though friends and people in my hometown didn't understand my situation, they cared about me. The doctor who was on call at the hospital came to the mental health clinic and spoke with me in the office. In just a few days, he would be the one to give my parents a diagnosis and who was very instrumental in my recovery.

I went into the office, and he began talking to me, asking some questions. He didn't get many answers that made much sense, and several times, he tried to make a phone call to see how I could get help. I remember acting silly, and unable to cooperate, and I repeatedly pushed the button down on the receiver and disconnected his phone call. He was tall, had a crew cut, and had glasses, and he wore a tannish tweed-like sports jacket. He didn't get angry with me but more frustrated and most likely annoyed.

Since mom was a registered nurse, I could go home until Monday morning. The doctor prescribed a medication to help me sleep, in hopes to manage the ecstatic moods. Being homecoming weekend, county fair week, and seeing the vibrant fall colors, I would describe this time of year for Lancaster as a jubilee weekend. Janice, my sister, was homecoming attendant, and her best friend, Jennifer, was queen.

My sister and Jennifer had been friends since middle school and then in high school were inseparable, fun, and popular. I loved Jennifer, and she was like a star to me. She sang beautifully and had the lead in every high school musical. She had a distinctive laugh, which was pretty. How do you describe a laugh? She sang soprano, so it was high and bubbly, and to me it went up and down like a wave in the ocean. Saturday evening was the homecoming dance, and my sister's date came over to the house. Janice's date, Mark, who later became her husband, wore a white suit and looked very nice. Jan looked so pretty, wearing a mint-green dress with a white blouse under it.

The remaining of the weekend was uneventful. Of course, our family didn't go anywhere like take a Sunday drive as we sometimes did. My parents were just taking care of me, continuing to worry and wonder what was wrong with me, and undoubtedly dreading the trip to the hospital and admission to the psychiatric unit. Today, I reflect back to how difficult that whole weekend was for my parents and perplexing to my brother and sister. This was only the beginning of an experience that you could call a journey and a nightmare, but I could never have known back then how it would change and mold me into the person I am today.

October 10

A Very Frightening Time for My Parents

This was the day that my parents took me to the hospital, but it wasn't an ordinary event; of course nothing was ordinary, normal, or healthy. Up until a few years ago, I thought my dad drove our black LTD with my mom in front and me in back. But a police officer actually drove our car with dad, mom and me as passengers. My dad told me since I was so hyper, he didn't want me jumping out of the car on the way to the hospital. The doors were locked, and so many years later after my father shared that with me, I couldn't believe it, but it made a lot of sense. I was very hyper and agitated, but he told me I was never mean or defiant. The drive to Riverside Methodist Hospital in Columbus took forty-five minutes.

I don't have a recollection of the actual admission to the hospital. I just know that my parents had to leave me there, and of course, I didn't understand, nor could I grasp it then, but I certainly can comprehend today how tough and painful that had to have been for them. Now, being an adult and a mother gives me wisdom and understanding, but never having personally gone through something like this with my children, surely limits my understanding.

"Authorized Medical Personnel only" was the name of the area where my room was. It was a securely locked unit with two doors. The doctor and the nursing staff would unlock the first door and then open the second door, where my room was. I was placed in a room where there was a small vinyl sofa. Initially a bed was in the room, but because of my inability to stay in the room and my nervousness, I stripped the whole bed: sheets, blanket, and pillowcase.

So here I am in a room with a small couch, on the ninth floor at a large hospital on the psychiatric unit. I was emotionally and mentally ill, and as strange as it is for me to write those words, mentally ill, I believe that it's even more difficult for some people today to hear, grasp, appreciate, and understand mental illness.

Consequently, back then, there wasn't a specific adolescent unit at Riverside Methodist Hospital which today is called the Ohio Health Riverside Methodist Hospital. It was one general floor with people of different ages. My parents went home, not yet having any answers to this peculiar, mysterious, and abnormal thing that was going on with me.

It was lunch time at this point, and the nurse aide brought my meal to me. It was a grilled cheese sandwich, potato chips, and grape juice, and some fruit. When you're sick, you don't want to eat. If it's a mental illness or a physical one, the appetite isn't there, at least that's how it was with me. The anxiety and restlessness were escalating, so even if I would have had an appetite, I'm pretty certain that physically, I would not have been able to sit still long enough, so eating was simply impossible.

By evening, I was upset and began, at that point, thinking, what am I doing here? Where are my parents? I'm locked up in this room with one window, looking down eight stories. That's how I saw it, and that's how it was. I aimlessly wandered around my room, constantly pushing the call light, asking the nurses any and every question I could. This was the only way I knew to make sense of this crazy world I had entered. The days were long and slowly turned into nights. I was still in an area where only authorized visits were given, and only family could visit.

An Answer but Much Uncertainty

October 16–23:

A week after my admission to the hospital, my doctor, the one who I saw at the mental health clinic in Columbus, gave a diagnosis with an explanation to my parents. My mom later told me that she had reluctantly, with fear, asked the doctor before he gave her a diagnosis. She began to ask if I had schizophrenia, but before she could complete her question he kindly interrupted and told her that it wasn't schizophrenia. My mom was relieved because schizophrenia, at that time, she knew was exceedingly difficult to treat or cure. The doctor then began explaining to my mother what my illness was. "Robin has a chemical imbalance called manic depression."

Bipolar disorder: bipolar disorder is a mental health condition that causes significant changes in mood, behavior, and energy levels. The mood swings that affect people with bipolar disorder can last for days, weeks or even several months. People in the hypomanic or manic phase of bipolar experience euphoria and exhilaration without external cause. They may be excited and energetic, but the high is often short lived. Though this may be considered a "good mood," it is often experienced with an intensity not common to people without the condition. Furthermore, after the manic state ends, people with bipolar disorder often experience a jarring downward spiral that results in depression. Mayo Clinic, February 16, 2021

In the late seventies, bipolar disorder was called manic depression. Although my mom didn't get a lot of comfort when the doctor told her what this creepy and chilling thing was, she was more at ease to at least have a name for the abnormal behaviors that she and my family had seen, beginning less than two weeks before.

Being a registered nurse who had worked in psychiatric nursing in the past, she understood enough about mental illness to comprehend it. When it's your daughter, that's a whole different story in which you enter into a very scary and strange world. So, understanding it becomes difficult and unbearable at times.

I began getting mail almost every day: cards, magazines, candy, stuffed animals, and more. Those gifts added so much color to my room, but I couldn't enjoy them because I was having side effects from the medication while the doctor was getting the dose regulated. I had blurred vision, difficulty in swallowing, and body tremors. So, these issues made it impossible to enjoy any gifts I received. I recall stacks of cards wrapped in rubber bands falling from the bed to the floor. I couldn't read them well as I was still pretty sick. These side effects sound bad, but the doctor and nurses and other medical staff were exceptional, and several blood draws were done, so they could adjust the medication dosage for my body to respond the right way.

My mom and the nurses posted all of the cards on the large windows for me and my family to see. My friends and other peers at school signed and mailed a large poster board that said to get well soon and other kind words of encouragement. My English teacher was in charge of that, and she wrote my name and address of the hospital on the chalk board in my English class so people could send cards.

Though it wasn't easy for me, it was more difficult for my parents and siblings as they continued to wait for my healing and recovery. There are many things I recall during this time that are very memorable to me. There was much concern about me not eating. The doctor wanted to insert a feeding tube, which my mother was against doing. There were a couple of times she brought me a hamburger, milk shake, and French fries, thinking that would help me eat and increase my appetite, and it did. But my doctor didn't want her to do that. He wanted me to eat on my own, but I wasn't.

My mother often found herself in a catch twenty-two with the medical staff. My sister, Janice, sat on the edge of the bed and fed me. At one moment, she turned away and her eyes were glossy with tears. She was an extremely caring big sister and, at seventeen, struggled to see me too sick to feed myself.

Another time my mom was frustrated with my doctor was when I told her my stomach hurt. She thought I had an ulcer. When she told him that, he didn't think I did, and she said

"These doctors think that every illness is just in your head as if nothing is physical!" Yes, I was mentally ill, but my illness affected me physically as well. Later, in my sophomore year of high school, I had an x-ray done and did indeed have an ulcer.

When I was getting a little stronger, Janice clipped my fingernails that I had always bitten, and filed and colored them. On a lighter note, and positive one, the medicine I was taking cleared my face, for I had a lot of pimples. My mom and I chuckled about that. Another sweet memory I remember is when one of the nurses came in my room. She was eight or nine months pregnant, and I wanted to give her a hug, but there wasn't any room between her baby and me! We laughed because I couldn't really hug her.

I was getting a little stronger and eating some but not much. I was allowed to walk out in the living area, sometimes alone and other times with a nurse. I wasn't supposed to go in the area where the nurse's stations were, but I didn't know that. I went up and tapped on the window and smiled and cheerfully said hi. The doctor later reprimanded me for that. He wasn't mean but made it very clear to me to not do it again and told me that the nurses are busy working, and I shouldn't be interrupting them.

It was about this time that I asked him about going home. I was better but still not really close to being discharged. As he sat on the edge of my bed with his crew haircut and glasses, I noticed his eyes got watery, and he rubbed one of them to keep from getting more emotional. Still composed, very professional, and very caring, he said in so many words that he would see about working on getting me home. He obviously couldn't give me a date. Meanwhile back home, I was told later that my neighbor, who lived across the street from my house, had been praying for me and she and others were amazed at the progress I was making.

CHAPTER 3

Glimmer of Hope Toward Recovery

Late October, Early November:

I got strong enough to be able to move into a room with a roommate. Her name was Beth, she was fifteen years old, and had brown hair. She was very hyper and wasn't supposed to have caffeine. She told me these things, and the nurse and doctor told her to stay on the unit, or to have someone accompany her if she were to leave the unit but to not leave by herself. She didn't listen well!

She was too assertive for me, and I was definitely the quieter and more reserved one between the two of us. I specifically remember her asking me how physical I had gotten with a guy! That was extremely awkward. I was fourteen years old, in the hospital for an emotional and mental issue, and obviously she was, as well. I, of course, didn't know any details about her situation. Her question made me feel uncomfortable, and awkward. I hadn't even been to my first high school dance! Needless to say, Beth and I didn't have a lot in common, but we ended up getting along pretty well.

Beth was discharged, and I got a new roommate named Jane. She was pretty, kind, and sweet, had blond hair, and was in her early to mid-thirties. She was on a strict diet to lose weight and drank a very small container of a liquid diet supplement, which reminds me today of a communion cup that is used in church. That's all she had, for three meals. I'm sure she was on a plan where solid foods were introduced after a certain amount of weight loss. I assumed she had depression. Dad told me that she wasn't just on a psychiatric unit to lose weight, that more was going on in her life, but being overweight can cause depression.

Here I was, wanting to have an appetite but had difficulty in eating, and she wanted to eat but had to drink her diet supplement. She was determined to lose weight. There were a few times I threw a lot of my food in the trash so it would look like I was eating. I didn't have an eating disorder, nor did I want to lose weight, but it was still difficult to eat. Swallowing was still tough, and my appetite wasn't good.

One evening, Jane was talking to her husband on the phone and asked me if I wanted to say hi to him. His name was Eric, so I walked over to her bedside and sat beside her. There wasn't much room for me to sit because of her weight problem, and she commented about that, feeling uncomfortable. She gave the phone to me, and Eric said hi and asked me how I was. He was very kind to me.

I sometimes wonder today how Jane is. She was so kind and caring to me and very positive about her health and weight-loss plan. Even though she didn't know why I was in the hospital, it's as if she did.

Jane was discharged, and then for the remaining time at the hospital, I didn't have a roommate. Each day I got stronger, and my appetite was improving. I was eating more and therefore gaining more strength and overall, feeling stronger physically. Life was more enjoyable, but I wasn't fully recovered, and I still didn't understand what had happened to me, or what bipolar disorder was. It would take a while before I could process all of the events that had occurred since mid-September. I was able to have visitors, besides family, come to see me. Close friends Kelli, Ann, and Mike visited me.

I continued getting stronger physically and mentally, walking in the living area without a nurse accompanying me. In order for me to continue making the progress and becoming more independent, I would walk to the medicine cart and take my medicine at the time needed. So, someone said something over the PA system like: "Patients on West Wing, medications are now being given." The "Mobile gift cart" was a mobile mini-store that a staff person would take on the unit, and you could buy something. There were many items on that cart, such as candy, gum, snack foods like potato chips and peanuts, and Doritos, a variety of crackers, stuffed animals, and other souvenir like things. It was very colorful. On one occasion, I ate lunch in the day room with the other patients, which was fun. One afternoon while having lunch, I was eating soup with crackers, then had to sneeze, and the crackers went everywhere!

I played bingo with the other patients and had occupational therapy. Doing occupational therapy had its good days and bad. The occupational therapist had me make a project in a room that looked like a combination of a shop class, and an art room that you see in high school. It was a large room, at least it looked big to me, and all the tools and art supplies hung on the wall. My project was a copper-colored aluminum butterfly, and I used art tools to design the details. There were projects that others made, and I remember seeing a clown that scared me. The colors and the smile the clown had on his face were creepy to me. That particular session was uncomfortable and overwhelming, so the therapist discreetly, with compassion, took me back to my room. Later, she had a session with me, and I completed the project. I didn't know at the time when I made that piece of art that I liked butterflies, but later discovered how much I enjoy and appreciate them, especially the Monarch ones.

CHAPTER 4

A Very Memorable and Special Visit

November 6:

One evening, my English teacher Ms. Speer, visited me and by this time I was able to have visitors and was feeling much better and heading in the right direction toward recovery. She was my favorite teacher whom I loved and admired. She was dedicated to teaching and had a distinct passion for teenagers.

That's how I remember her, but I will never forget this particular evening. She knocked on my door and came in carrying a colorful bag. "How are you?" she asked. Since she was kind, pleasant, and positive, it's as if a burst of sunshine followed right behind her. Delighted to see her, I said I was good and then she reached into her bag and pulled out a yellow rose and handed it to me. I don't remember how I replied, but I do remember how I felt—loved and cared for. Then she took out a red book with golden trim and handed it to me. Inside were white blank pages. She gave it to me and said, "This is yours on one condition: if you promise to share your good days with me."

My Introduction to Journaling

November 6:

Ms. Speer and everyone else, I feel great. I talked to a lot of people and felt so happy about possibly going home soon. I'm getting kind of tired now, but I'm so happy!

November 7:

Morning: I was feeling good this morning, and thinking about everybody at school. I feel quite well! I took my shower, and put my favorite blue outfit on. I didn't eat much for breakfast. The doctors are so cute! Thanks so much, Ms. Speer, for this book. I have to write this one more thing: I don't have any problems singing and writing or making up songs.

November 8:

I feel great this morning. Last night, I found out that I could have Ann and Kelli visit me, but it will be a surprise when they come. I'm happy but so tired. I stayed up and watched an Elvis Presley movie. I get to go home this Friday and stay through the weekend. Yay! I had a busy day. Kelli, Dad, and Janice came up and gave me some more presents.

Mom wrote that day: "Mom came in today." It was nice to see her. I had a pretty good day. Seeing her handwriting in my journal today, brings back memories of how she cared deeply about me getting well. I've been having a good time, though I'm very tired. My mental health was upsetting me, so I read a medical dictionary. I don't remember but I wanted to know more about why I was in the hospital, and what bipolar disorder was.

November 10:

I feel really upset because I'm not at home. I was crying, (depressed). They said they might be able to arrange that I can go home for good. Hopefully, I can. We'll see!

November 11:

I felt really good this morning. I got up at 8:00, took a shower and washed my hair. I leave this morning for a weekend visit.

November 12:

I had a wonderful day at home. I had tasty food and had people come over to the house to visit me. I went to Kings Department Store, Buckeye Mart, and Jeanesville. I got a purse, cuticle remover, Noxzema, and deodorant. I had so much fun! I was really tired but had a nice day and slept really well in my bedroom that has new paint, carpet, and bedding.

November 13:

Today, I'm going back to the hospital. (Boo!) No, I was excited. Lori and Mike, my friends came over to the house to visit me. I was so tired but had a good weekend. I slept on the way back to the hospital. I was exhausted and overwhelmed because of seeing many people, and I hadn't been anywhere except the hospital for over a month.

November 14:

I talked to my doctor, and I might be going home Wednesday (yay!) I called Mom. I had a good day. I'm so happy! That's all I have to say, except that I'm pretty happy about maybe going home for good on Wednesday.

November 15:

I get to go home Wednesday for sure! Mom called my doctor, and he said, "Yes." Ms. Speer came to see me, and I told her about my leaving the hospital, and she was really happy.

CHAPTER 5

Joy: Finally Going Home

November 16:

I'm going home today at 12:00. I told everybody at the hospital about my leaving. I packed and said goodbye to everyone. People hugged me and even told me I was the life of the party. I don't remember thinking that. I do recall thinking that others were the life of the party. Mom and I left with me forgetting my art project, the copper butterfly, but we didn't go back to get it. We got home at 3:00. It was raining, but we stopped and got my medicine and ate at Wendy's. I went to bed at 10:05, feeling so happy.

November 24:

Thanksgiving Day. I got up feeling well. Then we went to Grandma's home, and celebrated Thanksgiving. It was really good. We had Turkey, dressing, and the whole works. Then we went to Aunt Judy's lovely new home. I was so happy. At the end of the day, I was very tired. I had a crying spell over when I was sick. It was awful! Later, I felt better. It had been only eight days that I had been home from the hospital, so I was still recovering. My mom and doctor told me that if everyone were fully recovered before they were discharged from the hospital then the hospital would be overflowing.

I'm finally getting well. I'm going to get my ears pierced after Thanksgiving. I went to bed about 9:00. Every step of the way was new for me and my family, particularly my parents. I wrote this several times, not having any idea what "getting well" actually meant. I just knew that each week I felt stronger but what does that really mean when you're an adolescent and still trying to comprehend or grasp a diagnosis of bipolar disorder and many of the events that occurred prior to my hospital admission which was only six weeks ago.

December 7:

We didn't have school December 7–9, due to a lot of snow. My journal entries during these days were about school and some winter school events being cancelled and having difficulty in my Earth Science class. My English teacher was always supportive as I told her my frustrations with Earth Science. The teacher was a very good one, but that class was still very difficult for me.

A Needed but Unusual Vacation

Family vacation

December 17–28:

My family and I went to Fort Meyers and Cape Coral, Florida, during some of the Christmas vacation. These were the places we always went to on most of our family vacations, but this was the first time we went during Christmas time. This particular vacation was different because we were so used to seeing snow on Christmas day or at least sometime in December.

Seeing palm trees was nice, but the temperature during that time was in the upper sixties, so we didn't swim a lot, which all of us enjoyed doing, but we were together as a family, and that was important. Looking back, I'm pretty sure that my parents thought that this vacation would be good for me and our family after I was discharged from the hospital. We ended up going home earlier than planned since it was cold.

December 27:

We got up and left our hotel at 10:00. We went to Cape Coral and went to the Farrow's, home. Barb, Paul, her husband, and their two children, Jayne and Dan, are very close friends to my family. Barb Farrow was my mom's best friend. She and my mom met while they were in nurse's training. Barb and my mother stayed in touch through the years. Our families became close friends.

I have so many fun and wonderful memories of that family. Still today, Jayne and I and my sister laugh about the fun and crazy things we all did while being together. Swimming was definitely a fun necessity, for we all loved to swim and stay up late on Saturday evenings, playing hide and seek inside their home. Jayne, my sister, and I stayed up late laughing, and Paul repeatedly tried to be patient while telling us to go to sleep. Nobody was laughing much on Sunday mornings because Jayne couldn't wake up. Her dad had to use a fly swatter that he tapped on her back in order to get her to move!

But probably the craziest thing was when Janice, Dan, and Jayne were on the boat, and a tornado was sighted. They weren't in danger, but Jan jumped in the water! Dan who was normally very calm, became pretty nervous and concerned but he and Jayne did not jump ship! Today, we still talk, and laugh about that story.

CHAPTER 6

Adjustments, Family,
High School, and Loneliness

February 3, 1978:

I went to my Aunt Judy's home to spend the weekend. I had
fun. I spent a lot of time with my aunt and my cousin, her
son, Bret. We were very close. We all had such a nice time and
Judy was so kind and loving to me. One of my earliest memories with her and Bret is when I babysat Bret. Judy bought me a
bottle of Charlie Perfume, which is the kind she wore, as a gift
for babysitting him. I was twelve and he was four. I really liked
that perfume, so I was delighted when she bought it for me.

We shopped together, watched movies, spent time with
Judy's brother and his family and her sisters. I'll always remember
Judy liking Pepsi and peanuts, making lovely Christmas wreaths,
taking me shopping, and selling Mary Kay makeup. There were
many Sunday mornings when she made scrambled eggs, crispy
bacon, Pillsbury cinnamon rolls, and orange juice. These kinds
of weekends went on until I went to college.

February 6:

My day was bad. I haven't been feeling so great, and I don't have much ambition. Maybe because of this winter (cold and a lot of snow). I went swimming. I had a membership at the YMCA. This was a really wise and thoughtful thing my parents did for me simply because exercise helped me physically, emotionally, and mentally. Swimming was the exercise I did, and I loved to swim then and still do today.

February 11:

I went to work with Mom. It was boring. We ordered a pizza during her break time. This was the time my mother began occasionally taking me to work with her. I learned then but appreciated years later a lot about her sincere love, patience, and compassion that she had toward her patients.

She worked at a small hospital where the people were severely physically and mentally handicapped. All of her patients were born with these serious conditions. I went to work with my mom several times, and I admired her as she cared for those special people who ranged in ages from seventeen to sixty years old. I remember one particular man she was feeding, who required a feeding tube in order to get his nutrition. He had beautiful eyes, and I said to her one evening while I was at work: "It's sad." I said that because he was bed-bound and would need to live in the hospital the rest of his life. Her response was: "It's really not sad because that's all he knows." I thought he was about seventeen, but he was in his thirties. People like him who are severely mentally and physically handicapped look younger than they are because they don't live in the world, work, or have the good and bad stresses of life. That's always been very intriguing to me.

I didn't know it at the time but looking back, perhaps my mom was conscientiously instilling in me traits of compassion and patience for sick people. Later, when I was seventeen, she told me, "I think you would be good at working in a nursing home." That went over really well! I think I either said no way or looked at her like she was crazy. Well, when I was twenty-three, I worked at a nursing home during the summer and learned that I had compassion for the patients who had dementia, or mental illness. At that time, that work experience was sad and disturbing to me.

March 10:

It was a wonderful day. Mary and I went to see the movie *Heroes*. It was really good. We also went to Town and Country restaurant and got a sandwich. Mary was in my high school class and was truly kind, smart, and seemed socially comfortable and confident in being her own person in that she didn't follow the crowd. She and I got together several times, and she occasionally spent the night at my house. She knew how to be a loyal friend.

March 27:

I got 110 percent on my vocabulary test in English. I didn't even cheat! (Just kidding, I wouldn't do that). Mom thinks all of my friends have turned on me because they never call me. I don't think they have. Adolescence is a crazy time for any teenager. I had a nice crowd of friends, but after I got out of the hospital, I changed, and we went our separate ways. My best friend, Kelli, told me forty years later how she felt so badly about the whole situation and not understanding it as a teenager. She said, "All I knew was my best friend was gone." When you're fourteen or fifteen, you can't understand yourself, much less try to grasp your friend's experience with bipolar disorder.

May 4:

I was kind of down during first, second, and third periods, but later felt better. Tomorrow is our singing ensemble program at Tarhe Elementary School, and I'm excited. Singing was the one thing I loved any time, whether it be at home, school, or during school concerts. It was very therapeutic throughout all four years of high school. I would often listen and sing along to music from The Sound of Music, South Pacific, Oklahoma, as well as songs by the Carpenters, and many other songs from my favorite albums.

CHAPTER 7

A New Phase in My Life

I began writing in my second journal. Ms. Speer who visited me while I was in the hospital gave it to me, and inside of both journals are name plates that say: "From the library of." I signed my name in each of those. The first name plate had a picture of two monarch butterflies. The second had a picture of a blue ocean with high waves.

Lancaster County Fair

October 11:

I got up about 9:30; we left to pick up Mary and got there about 11:00. We watched some bands, and I saw some former teachers, other students from Fisher Catholic High School, and kids from Lancaster High School. Patty, Mary, and I ran around most of the day but only rode one ride. I got some fudge and a homemade chicken sandwich that the Lancaster band booster parents made, and some chicken noodle soup. We left about 4:30. I called Janice at college. I was in such a great mood.

Everything is going smooth sailing, finally! I could always call my sister when I felt great, and life was going well; or when life was tough, and I felt awful. She was always supportive and hasn't changed. This particular moment in high school (my sophomore year) was very positive because I felt like I was really starting to enjoy school and life again. Lancaster County Fair was a fun time in our town. It was a time when you saw many friends. Today, it reminds me of a large family reunion which a small town like Lancaster offers.

January 1, 1979:

Happy New Year, I'm sorry that I didn't write. I thought I would just wait until I was feeling better to resume my journal. When there was a gap in my writing, it was sometimes because of feeling down about life, for example, if I didn't make a singing group or my peers or friends were acting distant toward me. I think back then, I wanted to be part of a group or a click. My social group that began in seventh grade had drastically changed, and life wasn't the same for me after the onset of bipolar disorder and being in the hospital. My friends that I had beginning in high school were typical teenagers in many ways, wanting to be with a group of friends. But I learned later that even in high school, traumatic events and serious illnesses that happen often cause you to look at life differently. You mature at a different rate than your peers. That was the case for me, but of course, then I didn't appreciate or understand that.

April 20, 1980:

Today was a really special day in my life. It was Youth Sunday at our church, and I, among others, gave a mini sermon. It was more like a speech, and I got a lot of compliments and felt really good about it. Mom, Dad, Grandma, and Grandpa were there and were really proud of me. I especially liked getting attention or recognition. Mom told me something that I really liked hearing: I could write my thoughts and feelings well.

I have to write when I'm depressed because it makes me feel better. I guess you could say writing the speech and people complimenting me makes me feel better about wanting to lose weight. No, I haven't lost anymore, and it really tears me up inside, but I am the only one who can do this. I'll try again tomorrow. I don't have that much confidence in myself, and I feel lost, insecure, and discouraged. It just interrupts my life. I even avoid seeing people because I feel self-conscious. Mom is taking me to a doctor to get some blood work done, and I'll find out what my weight is, which will embarrass me to death! Hopefully, I'll get on a good diet.

My life has changed so much, and my social life isn't very good, but it has improved. I want to change myself so badly, but I don't think I have the strength. I want so much to be thin again, but it is the most difficult thing in my life right now. My weight fluctuated beginning in ninth grade. One reason was because my doctor prescribed a different medication, which had a side effect of weight gain, and I wasn't active like I had always been. To be at a healthy weight, I needed to lose twenty-five pounds. My family doctor suggested a healthy, calorie-based diet, and exercise. I lost the weight in six months by following a healthy diet and walking home from the high school almost every day, which was a three-mile walk.

April 22:
Well, I want to write more of my thoughts and feelings because I want to compare them later with other ones. I walked home from school today and I'll continue doing that. It's a long walk, but it's worth it. I'm proud to say that I have stuck to my

diet for two days, and I feel strong and encouraged. Dad and I went to the basketball game. I started thinking about feeling insecure and lonely and how I have no confidence in myself. I had some tears, and Dad listened and cared. Then I began thinking about the junior prom and how I'm not going. After the game, I went to the library to study for a big history test and later felt better. Dad was a good listener when I had days or moments when my confidence was shaken. He may not have always had answers, though at times he did. Still, he cared and supported me.

August 24:

Well, summer is over, so school will be starting soon. I went to Sunday school, which was fun. Then I picked up one of my friends, and we went to her church. It was different than what I was used to hearing in my church. Then later, we went to the evening service. A gospel singing group sang, and they preached beliefs we didn't like. Another one of my friends and I talked about her church, and we had an argument. She said the people believed you could get saved from your sins every week. I didn't fully understand what getting saved meant, but what my friend said didn't make sense to me. How could you go to the altar, I said, and accept Jesus, but then live the rest of the week sinning and attend church the next Sunday, and go to the altar and get saved again? The concept of "Getting saved" was new to me.

September 4:

It's the first day of school, and I'm so happy to be a senior. I think it's going to be a great year! Tryouts for Singing Gales is in a couple of days, and I really want to be in this singing group.

I'm praying this: Oh God, and Jesus, give me the relaxation that I need to make this singing group. I've tried so hard to show people that I can sing. Help me to be calm and to remember if I don't make it, then allow me to simply be thankful for the audition. Oh God, I want this so badly. I didn't even know much about Jesus except that he was the son of God, born on Christmas Day, and died on the cross.

September 6:

Well, tryouts for Singing Gales went well; however, I didn't make it. I was really upset, but shortly got over it. Mom got me a yellow rose and a card since I was feeling bad about not making the singing group. The card said, "You can't appreciate success until you've had some failures. You should have a great womanhood." I kept that little card that came with the rose in my purse for several years. Mom validated my disappointment by giving me the card and the rose. I quit my job at Taco Bell because the assistant manager was so mean and unreasonable. My manager called me and apologized and said, "Whenever I go away something bad happens with this assistant manager." Her understanding of the situation made me feel better.

September 17:

Today was my best day for schoolwork and feeling well physically and mentally. Oh, I made Symphonic Choir! Our choir director told me that the Singing Gales tryout was my entrance into Symphonic Choir. I was so happy, and he told me that my voice is better suited for this particular choir. Later in the spring, I was so glad to have gotten a superior grading at a solo singing competition that was at Capital University. A select group from symphonic choir participated in this.

October 20:

I had a wonderful day. I only hope that this year doesn't get boring due to my lighter schedule of classes. I'm ready for my accounting test, and if I get two A's, then I'll have a B average in the class. I'm so happy right now. Thank you, God, for making me quite different than others. Thank you for that special something in me that says be different because you are, and you are not a conformist. You can be happy without a drug or being a phony person. Just be yourself. I didn't realize or really comprehend then that the hospital experience and being diagnosed with bipolar disorder would have a monumental impact on my life. This was only the beginning.

November 17:

We had a big snow, which was the first one, and I love it! *The Diary of Anne Frank* is on TV right now. It's very sad. Sometimes I wonder if my journals will ever be published. I have been keeping a diary, or journal, since my first year of high school. Soon I'll be on the fourth one.

CHAPTER 8

A Very Unexpected Journey

December 4:

This day was the worst! At school today, some kids at lunch were saying false things about one of my friends, and if we would have been somewhere other than school, I think I would have smacked the person who said the cruel comment. Then I got home and worked on my accounting. That class is so difficult. I felt terrible, but I couldn't cry. So, I went to church early for choir practice and went to the sanctuary. I prayed, but it was difficult to concentrate. I only wish I could understand or know Jesus Christ more clearly in my life.

I went to church a few times with my boyfriend, but didn't hear any sermons. I didn't know a lot, but I knew the church service was strange, and I didn't care for it. I came home one night and opened a very old King James Bible that my mom gave to me and glanced at it, but I didn't read any Bible verses.

Losing Two Friendships, Beginning the Path of Deep Depression

January 12, 1981:

Well, a lot has happened, I mean a lot. The reason I haven't been writing is because something really terrible happened. Nancy's mother called me on Sunday and told me that Nancy and I can't be friends and hang around together anymore. That previous Friday, she and another friend and I went out, and I had one beer, and later Nancy's mom smelled it on my breath. She accused me of many wrong things. Oh, it was terrible! Oh, how I hate what Nancy's mother did! When I saw Nancy at her locker this morning, she was so upset that her hands were trembling. It was the worst thing in my life. Something good happened: I got accepted into Muskingum College, but something else bad happened. My boyfriend broke up with me. I've been depressed.

January 25:

My life has been empty and depressing. That's why I haven't been writing. I miss my best friend and boyfriend. They were my friends, and now I can't talk to anybody, so I thought I should write about it. School is boring, and I feel insecure and most of all very lonely. I know somewhere in all of this mess, God has a reason for these bad things to happen. I have never hurt so badly. The musical tryouts are tomorrow, and I hope I get an important part. I've been getting sick of church choir, which isn't like me. I'm so tired of Lancaster, and I want to go to college right now and forget these things that have recently happened, and my past. Janice is home from college, taking a break. She and Dad and I went to Grandma's house today. Then I went to youth group, and it was fun. I've been reading the Bible to help me feel better. I believe it's helping me. Not realizing it then, I was experiencing mild to moderate depression. My senior year began so well. I was happy, doing well in my classes, and enjoying Symphonic Choir, and loved our Christmas program which was like a small musical. Everything was going great, but now I was experiencing depression. This was the beginning of something different than what happened to me in ninth grade that would change my life forever.

January 27:

I made the chorus for the musical. This day was boring. The only thing that went well was my accounting test. Well, I have never cried about these terrible things yet, but this evening, I just had to let it out (Losing my best friend and boyfriend). My life is so empty without her and her friendship. She was my one best friend, and I feel absolutely awful!

March 8:

It's been a while since I have written but not much has changed in my life. I got asked to the senior prom, and I said yes, but I am not excited about it. I figure I should continue writing in my journal. Just because something bad happens to me, doesn't mean I have to quit my life. I'm lonely and sad but need to write in this book.

CHAPTER 9

Plummeting into the Depths of the Deepest Depression

April–June 1981:

The depression was getting worse each month. I quit writing in my journal during this time. Looking back, one evening in late June 1981, I had a very serious conversation with my mother, one which I will always remember and which was an extremely critical moment in my life. She was in the kitchen, sweeping the floor. The summer was unbearably difficult for me. After Christmas of 1980, my condition worsened as I plummeted into a deep depression and felt as if I could not get above the sinking waters in which I was drowning. I sat down at the kitchen table and said to her: "Mom, I can't do this."

She responded, "What do you mean"?

I said, "I don't want to live."

I didn't use the word suicide, but I wanted to take my life and had been mentally obsessed with it for several weeks.

"Robin, I thought that's what you were going to say but don't do that. You have so much going for you."

"Mom, I don't feel that, even though people say that to me."

She responded by saying, "Let me tell you something about my life. I see you are like me in some ways. When I was young, I was quiet and didn't have a lot of friends. But then when I went to nurse's training, I made good friends, and found my niche." I think that will happen to you when you go to college."

I listened and then we talked about the psychologist I had seen a couple of times earlier that summer. He said I wasn't depressed and that I needed to relax and get more sleep, but nothing was farther from the truth. I didn't want to get out of bed in the mornings, even though I slept eight to ten hours most nights.

My dad found it strange that I wanted to go to bed at 8:00 at night when I was seventeen years old. Concerned, and perplexed, he once said, "It seems abnormal for you to go to bed at 8:00 since you're a teenager." This depression was unlike the initial bipolar experience in ninth grade. There were few manic episodes rather an extremely dark and unexplainable long season in my life. We finished the conversation by my mom stating with determination, "We're getting a different doctor." Janice, my sister, and Jimmy, my brother, tried to help me with the depression. I recall one evening telling my sister how the darkness was getting worse, but I didn't share with her about wanting to take my life. Jimmy kindly tried to encourage me when I was very upset and struggling with memory lapses, difficulty with my thought processes, and my very low confidence level. He said, "Robin, I think you think clearly," as he sincerely tried to boost my confidence. Being a high school teacher, teaching health and fitness, and a physical education teacher, he introduced jogging to me, thinking it would help. I tried but didn't continue. I didn't share with him my thoughts on taking my life.

My mom did what she said. She made an appointment with a doctor in early July. His office was located in Zanesville, Ohio, which was conveniently located about thirty minutes from Muskingum College. As my mom and dad and I drove that day to the doctor's office, my dad asked me, "Do you have any hope?"

"No," I replied. I couldn't imagine or even comprehend feeling better because I had been in this state of depression for several months. If I would not have had this conversation with my mother and her getting the right psychiatrist, I'm certain I would have taken my life. To this day, I don't know if my mom shared with my dad that serious conversation back in the summer of 1981.

The medicine my doctor in Zanesville prescribed was lithium, which was the same medication that was used to treat me when I had the initial onset of bipolar disorder. During this visit with the doctor on that summer day back in July, my dad said to him: "We just want Robin to get back to her down-to-earth self again." Many years later, in 2017, while visiting him, I sat in his living room that day and told him how I valued what he said and never realized he understood and deeply cared about me. He wasn't expecting that conversation and it was an emotional and special moment for both of us.

Hope Found

November 15, 1981:
A new Life a new beginning
Oh, How I can love the Lord
And feel His love and beauty once more.
No more depression, no more sadness,
Finally, a life of only contentment and confidence.
A new life a new beginning. Oh, how I can
Feel His love and beauty once more.

I am now in college, and the above writing expresses my feelings, and I still cannot write enough about how I feel and how relieved I am. About the last time I wrote in my journal, it was a time when I found myself in an extremely serious and hopeless depression. It led me to impaired thinking with memory lapses and eventually an obsessive contemplation with suicide.

I had this deep depression for six months, which actually began in December, 1980 but plummeted deeper until July, 1981. I felt miserable, isolated, and scared. This depression affected my whole being: my social life, my academics, my job and so many other things.

The main issue was: How do you tell someone like your boss or your teacher that you can't think or remember things when you're seventeen years old? I lost the summer job I had because I couldn't concentrate. I was dysfunctional, and it's as if I had no feelings. It was miserable, like I was living in a horrible nightmare!

My parents gave to the doctor my history of bipolar disorder, my 1977 hospital stay, and the medication, lithium, that my first doctor prescribed. It didn't take this doctor long to tell my parents that I had a mood disorder. Within three days after resuming lithium I felt amazingly different. I didn't just have a ray of hope, I had a new lease on life, which I did not have a few hours prior to walking into the doctor's office. I was in a serious and deep depression for eight months and felt back to being myself in only three days thanks to lithium working for me!

My dad asked me a few days after my doctor's appointment if I felt better, and I said yes. "Robin feels better!" I heard him telling my mom. This was a family illness. All of us were affected by this, but by the time I left for college on August 29, I was mentally and physically stronger and healthy again.

Chapter 10

Muskingum College, 1981–1982

C ollege life for me at Muskingum College was a very positive experience in many ways. It was a time to begin a new season in my life. I met a lot of people and made good friends, and I was able to enjoy it because I was no longer in a deep depression, but academically, I struggled at times. It was difficult for me to organize my time, with a studying schedule and developing a routine. My grades in my freshman year varied. In some classes I got average grades, some above average, and one class below average. Though I was very conscientious, there were times when I didn't get the proper amount of sleep, but that is typical for a lot of college students. For me, however, I needed to get an adequate amount of sleep to keep my moods balanced. My medication was effective, but I would stay up too late sometimes, studying or socializing. Looking back, I wasn't ready to attend college at that time. I was ready to experience a new life: physically, mentally, and emotionally, but not academically.

A Unique Invitation to the Bible

I loved swimming but missed the opportunity to swim on the team in high school. There was a conflict in my schedule in that I was in the musical, and practices for both activities were at the same time. I was glad to have the opportunity to swim on the team at Muskingum College. The swim coach requested the team return from Christmas vacation a few days early to practice for an upcoming swim meet. I did, and one cold snowy evening I was in my dorm room where it was very quiet. The resident director came in and suggested to me that during this time when most students were still on Christmas vacation, it was a good time to draw closer to God and read the Bible. I didn't really understand but took her advice, so that evening I read some of Psalms, but didn't think seriously about what I read.

The first semester of my sophomore year was more difficult than my last semester as a freshman. My grades were not good, having a C or D average in some classes, other classes a B, and one class I was failing. I was placed on academic probation. After a discussion with my parents and a desire on my part, I transferred to Ohio University, Lancaster's branch. So, I began the winter semester at home. The change initially was difficult. I missed my friends at Muskingum College, and it was an adjustment living at home after being on my own for a year and a half. Classes went better for a while.

CHAPTER 11

A Desire to Thank Someone, and the Path to a Saving Faith

January 11, 1983:

*L*ord, I need some guidance through this change in my life right now. I can't do it alone, so with your wisdom, help me to understand and accept these changes, and Lord, teach me to never fail in seeing your beautiful creation that surrounds me.

I was attending Ohio University's Lancaster Branch and met a guy at college, and we shared similar interests. We were compatible and enjoyed each other's company, but in less than a year discovered we didn't have as much in common as we thought, so we stopped dating. It was at this time that I felt really lonely and still occasionally missed some of my friends at Muskingum College. I wasn't a religious person, but I prayed to God. I was searching for a peace and strength to help me deal with the changes of transferring to a different college.

April 19, 1983:

I thank God for the trees, animals, and beautiful mountains. I thank Him for the people and those who bring joy into my life. I thank Him for the strength He gives when times get so difficult and discouraging. I thank God for giving us His Son to save us. Like a child who is doing well, but desires to further his knowledge or use his imagination, I long to become more spiritually enlightened through God's teachings.

I wrote the above writing because I was so thankful and happy to be mentally, physically, and emotionally well again. I had a sincere need to thank someone. So, I sent a letter to an English teacher that I had when I was a senior in high school and my doctor in Zanesville, thanking them and telling them that I was in college and free from the deep depression. My doctor already knew how I had recovered from the deep depression, but I wanted to tell him that I was in college, and life was going well. This former English teacher took time during his break to help me with algebra. (An English teacher helping me with algebra!) This teacher was not the one who gave me my first journal when I was a freshman in high school and in the hospital. It was about this time that I met David at Ohio University's branch, and we became friends and began dating. He invited me to the church where he and his family attended. It was there where I began to learn about God and Jesus and the gospel.

May 14, 1983:

I'm ready to learn about accepting and trusting Jesus Christ into my heart. It will take a while, I suppose. Oh God, I am searching for something higher in life than just physically living. I long to learn about following Your Son, Jesus Christ. I have the desire, oh Lord, and I believe you will guide me and show me the truth. "Ask and it will be given to you, seek and you will find; knock and the door will be opened to you. For everyone who asks receives; the one who seeks finds; and to the one who knocks, the door will be opened" (Matt. 7:7–8).

A Long-Desired Gift

August 20:

"Therefore, if anyone is in Christ, the new creation has come. The old has gone, the new is here!" (2 Cor. 5:17).

During a special church service, Barbara, David's mother, prayed with me. I still remember her kind, sweet, and gentle voice as she came up to me while I knelt at the altar, and placed her hand on my shoulder and said, "Robin?" Then she prayed with me, and that evening, I received Jesus Christ as my Lord and Savior.

I soon discovered that it didn't take any time to learn about trusting Jesus Christ into my heart. I simply had a desire to know Him, and He chose me! It's so amazing to think that on December 4, 1980, I wrote in my journal, "I only wish I could understand or know Jesus Christ more clearly in my life." That was the last sentence I wrote before I plunged into a deep depression.

I really liked going to church where David introduced me to many people who demonstrated love, kindness, and sincerity in their walk with God. I'm grateful for David who first invited me to church and shared the gospel with me. I also loved and appreciated his parents, Tom and Barbara. Marla, David's sister, became a special friend to me. She played the piano naturally, and beautifully, and accompanied me when I sang two songs that I wrote and sang in church on several occasions.

Marla played by ear and wrote the arrangement of the songs that we shared with the congregation several times during worship. The songs I wrote were called: "Morning Afternoon and Evening" and "Jesus Is My Peace." I had many Sunday meals with David, his parents, and Marla and her husband, Raphael, who were often there. They were like a second family to me. I attended church there for five years. Other people I met and became friends with were Lisa and Mark, Belva, Emi, Cyndi, and many others. Their families who were very kind and loving. I had been seeking to know God. I asked, and I received. He chose me! "For He chose us in him before the creation of the world to be holy and blameless in his sight. In love he predestined us for adoption to sonship through Jesus Christ, in accordance with his pleasure and will-to the praise of his glorious grace, which he has freely given us in the one he loves." Ephesians 1:4–6.

November 19:

Nothing stays forever except the Lord. He never fails you or deserts you but is always there when you trust Him and open your heart to receive His love and forgiveness of your sins. If you love the Lord with all of your heart and obey His word, then joy and peace are found.

Jesus replied, "Love the Lord with all your heart and with all your soul and with all your mind" (Matt. 22:37).

CHAPTER 12

Continual Struggles in College

December 7, 1984:

I've been depressed lately. My grades came in the mail, and once again, they were bad. I feel like I want to quit college and find a job that is related to my interests. It is a relief just thinking that there may be something for me besides college, and then I might not have so much pressure. It seems like 80 percent of my pressure comes from school. I have good parents, a nice home, and good friends. What else is there, but college to worry about, which seems to create problems in my life. Who knows, but the Lord? Time will tell. I was still taking classes part time at Ohio University Lancaster's campus but continued to have a difficult time maintaining average grades in each class. I did fairly well in some, but there was always one or two which I had difficulty.

December 29:

Today is the first day of a new life for me. I am not going to school next quarter. My doctor and I have finally gotten some-where with this situation. I'm not sure what I will do, so I'm nervous but relieved. My parents said it was okay if I didn't want to go to college, which really helped me not to feel the pressure I had been experiencing.

January 2, 1985:
Because I wasn't going to school next quarter and wasn't sure what I was going to do with my life, I wrote the following entry.

Oh, Lord,
I am so emotionally weak right now. Be my strength, God, as You walk with me.

I'm scared, God, and I'm afraid that all of my dreams are falling apart. Help me, Father, and strengthen my faith and show me that I haven't been dreaming or living in a fantasy world.

You are my strength, Lord, and without You, my life would be more chaotic than what it is now.

Help me with patience, endurance, and faith in a new year and a new beginning. Be with me, Father, as I walk into a time of uncertainty of not knowing what my desires and strengths are. Most important, Lord, give me an understanding of the days ahead.

"Trust in the LORD with all your heart and lean not on your own understanding; but in all your ways submit to him, and he will make your paths straight" (Prov. 3:5–7).

Unknown Medical Territory

January 9, 1985:

*A*fter much thought and earnest prayer from a few close friends, I decided to stop taking my medication. I want to make it clear that I am not saying for others who have bipolar disorder or other forms of depression to not take medication or stop taking it. I'm not against using medication. I struggled many times with serious mood swings during this time, as some of my writings show, but God was always with me and led me through unhealthy mood swings. I simply wanted to trust in God and, at that time, believed He would heal me. A lot of my writings were ones where I was strong and content, but there were others when my moods were erratic and upsetting. My family saw the highs and lows, particularly my parents and my sister. Later, I thought that I was healed but later discovered that wasn't true, or medically correct. But what was true then and remains true today is that God was always with me and that will never change.

"Have I not commanded you? Be strong and courageous. Do not be frightened, and do not be dismayed, for the LORD your God is with you wherever you go" (Josh. 1:9).

I think that keeping a journal where I could write my feelings, experiences about people, places, events, and anything I wanted was incredibly beneficial and therapeutic for me. Most important, I wrote about God after I trusted and received Jesus Christ into my life. God gave me faith to believe that He was always with me.

January 15:
"For I know the plans I have for you declares the LORD, plans to prosper you and not to harm you, plans to give you hope and a future. Then you will call on me and pray to me, and I will listen to you. You will seek me and find me when you seek me with all your heart" (Jer. 29:11–13).

I have such a relief in my heart and life right now, that I am not taking the lithium. It is really a pleasant change. I thank you, God, for You have answered my prayers in ways that I never dreamed. You are amazing, God, because of Your love to me and forgiveness when I sin. I want to trust that the plans You have for me are wonderful.

Complete Assurance That I Am a Child of God

February 18:
It's been a while since I have written in my journal, and I have so much to be thankful for. I know this: I am saved; it is no longer a feeling or mood that comes and leaves me. Through the doubts and fears, I still know that I am a child of God.
"The spirit Himself testifies with our spirit that we are God's children" (Rom. 8:16).

CHAPTER 14

Challenges, Peace, and Joy from Not Taking Medication

March 23:

*W*ithout the lithium these days, life is a little difficult. I get upset and my moods are erratic, and I know that people can't make me happy. I can't expect a guy to "make me happy." I will just have to control the mood swings, and I know it's not easy, but I will have to change my job or something else in my life. God will help me, but I must remember not to dwell on my sadness and to slow down when my moods begin to spiral in the wrong direction. God, help me.

"If you believe, you will receive whatever you ask for in prayer" (Matt. 21:22).

March 26:
It's a beautiful cool spring morning—a new beginning and a new season! Thank you, Lord, for peace, love, and restoration. A brisk but sunny and vibrant morning led me to a bike ride.

It's a good time to think, see, and believe that my life is going to change and the Lord will take my sadness and lessen the mild depression. I want to be happy, and at peace with my thoughts, and I want to be strong during my weak times. You, Lord, will be my guide and security in these days ahead.

"But he said to me, my grace is sufficient for you, for my power is made perfect in weakness. Therefore, I will boast all the more gladly about my weaknesses, so that Christ's power may rest on me" (2 Cor. 12:9).

Chapter 15

A Deep Yearning to Share the Gift; Refreshing and Wonderful Job Change

Peace, I leave with you; my peace I give you. I do not give to you as the world gives. Do not let your hearts be troubled and do not be afraid. (John 14:27)

April 15:

*G*od, You helped me through another rough time because I prayed and talked to You. I am thankful, Lord, and have a heart of peace and gratitude. The amazing thing that I know is this: If I have another trial, You will undoubtedly be here and give me peace. Help me to love You and others and to endure all situations in my life. God has certainly blessed me in so many ways. It's as if I received one thousand golden coins, falling off the trees like leaves! I never thought this problem of depression would go away naturally but I know it can with God's healing power and love. The Bible doesn't lie, and if others read His Word to discover that the answer to everything is in the Bible, then I believe they would be amazingly changed. Lord, guide me to another person, for I need to share my golden treasure that you have graciously given to me. I genuinely believe and know that after the serious state of depression I experienced in my last year of high school, God instilled in me an appreciation for life, a gift of peace and joy that would always be mine.

April 26:

I shouldn't spend precious time pondering on why You chose me, rather I should spend time telling others about You, and how great it is to be Your child and have assurance that You chose me to live for You and serve You.

"You did not choose me, but I chose you and appointed you so that you might go and bear fruit-fruit that will last. Then the Father will give you whatever you ask in my name. (John 15:16).

Understanding Grace and Forgiveness

God, there was a time that I thought it was impossible to serve You after I failed You, yet You continuously lift me up and tightly hold my hand through the shifting sands on which I stand. Thank you for leading me in the right direction. You are the right way, the only way, and I'm so glad You are with me every step of the way. I didn't have a clear understanding of God's grace and forgiveness when I wrote this entry and periodically I struggled with my sins.

"If we confess our sins, he is faithful to forgive us our sins and purify us from all unrighteousness" (1 John 1:9).

July 19:

Once again, I am in God's place of solitude, a place where my whole being has needed to be for a long time. God, please show me how to write again, for the world and my work schedule has so preoccupied me that I need this time alone, with peace, to simply write. God, thank you so very much for bringing me to this park where I can be alone with You. When will I be free from this schedule of confusion and anxiety? Please teach me to appreciate the trials I am experiencing because I know that strength and joy will come to me and give me a patient heart to trust You and believe in You. I remember waiting for years to feel happiness and peace in my heart and security in my life. Why, Lord, must I feel afraid and lonely when I only need to wait a short time to see a change in my life? And then, Lord, back when I was so very alone and sad, I didn't know You! Show me, Lord, to be patient as I wait for You.

"But those who hope in the Lord will renew their strength. They will soar on wings like eagles; they will run and not grow weary; they will walk and not be faint" (Isa. 40:31).

I was waiting to see if I was going to get a job as a teacher's aide at a school in Lancaster called Forest Rose. This was a school where physically and mentally challenged students attended. I really liked my job at Gloria Marshall's fitness salon, but the hours during the summer were split shifts: (8–12 and 4–8, and sometimes just four hours a day). I was looking for something else and really wanted to help special children. A few years back, I had volunteered at a center where children had cerebral palsy and really liked it, so Forest Rose seemed like a great place to work. I got a position, but it was a substitute one with only a few hours a week, so I worked there for a brief time.

August 8:

I will be finished working at Gloria Marshalls on August 24 on a full-time basis. God has given me a great change, a new job. On Monday, August 26, I will begin teaching a small, combined group of kindergarteners and first graders at Fairfield Christian Academy. I'm excited and grateful to God for this job and answer to prayer.

Working at Fairfield Christian Academy for three years was so rewarding and enjoyable. I loved my students and will always deeply appreciate the many experiences, challenges, and fun times I had with them and the other teachers. The teaching aspect was gratifying and it was exciting to see five- and six-year-olds learn. The beautiful part was teaching them about God, and His plan of salvation. I thank God for being able to make a difference in their lives, and they were definitely a blessing to me!

A Growing Faith and Understanding the Suffering of Others

August 15:

"Praise be to the God and father of our Lord Jesus Christ, the Father of compassion and the God of all comfort, who comforts us in all our troubles, so that we can comfort those in any trouble with the comfort we ourselves receive from God" (2 Cor. 1:3–4).

I ended up keeping my job at Gloria Marshall's and worked part time in the evenings and some weekends while teaching at the Christian school. I wrote the following writing when I stayed at one of my customer's homes whom I met while working. She wanted me to watch her cat while she was on a short vacation. I was watching television one evening and heard a sad and compelling story about a woman suffering from anorexia nervosa. I felt so sorry for her, so I wrote about her and the story she shared.

I don't know where you live, I've only seen your face and I don't remember your name, but I heard you cry out for peace and stronger health in your life. Your cry was not in those exact words, but your heart revealed a longing for those things. I don't know who is loving you if anyone is. They don't understand and are not able to deal with the problem. In just the few words that you said, the sadness in your heart and your crying, you revealed enough to me. Of course, God has always known your pain and suffering.

> Give it all
> Give it all
> Give it all to God

You need not explain, for we all need His love and power to save and change our lives. It doesn't matter what the problem is; He can take care of it and ease the pain in your body mind, and soul. You said the kind of life you had was "hell," the feeling of hopelessness. You revealed a need to have a healthier life, a more peaceful one. You don't know what to do or where to begin. I heard you seeking answers from the world and those answers aren't the ones you need.

> Give it all
> Give it all
> Give it all to God.

And He will, yes, He certainly will give you answers, and everything you need to make you the healthy person and beautiful woman that God intends for you to be. I know because He gave it to me. God can save you from all the pain that you feel in your body and all of the fear and loneliness that you may be hiding. So, I am going to pray for you in hopes that you will listen and discover the peace and love of God through His Son, Jesus Christ. I may never meet you, but God is telling me to carry or share this load with you as Jesus did when He suffered and died on the cross for you. The compassion and love I felt for this young woman did not come from me personally ever having the illness that she had. I just understood sadness and suffering that I had experienced. She was so honest in her need to be healthy and overcoming her problem.

August 18:

A Prayer by the Maple Trees

Love the LORD your God with all your heart and with all your soul and with all your strength. (Deut. 6:5)

Therefore, put on the full armor of God, so that when the day of evil comes, you may be able to stand your ground, and after you have done everything, to stand. (Eph. 6:13)

Take the helmet of salvation and the sword of the spirit,
which is the word of God. (Eph. 6:17)

God, This is such a beautiful morning, with all of your freshness and radiant sun, which surrounds my mind, body, and soul.
In front of me stands three beautiful maple trees, all different
but created by You, Lord, who are powerful and amazing. Are
there any leaves on these trees that have the same pattern, the
same number of prongs stemming from them? As I pray to You
in thanks of this glorious morning, I write five prayers to You:
First, I promise to love You God, through every path which
is ahead of me, and through the trials of hopeless moments,
peaceful, and joyous ones. Second, I want to love my friends
and pray for my enemies. Third, I want to serve You with all
my heart and do Your will. Fourth, Lord, I want to resist the
enemy and his ways for he knows my weaknesses, and I am
sometimes ignorant of his power. As you continue to give me
wisdom, Lord, I need to stand tall and fight against him with the
sword of the spirit. Fifth, Lord, is the last promise and the most
important one: The fact that You sent Your Son, Jesus Christ
to die for my sins, I now have peace and joy on the earth and
some day in heaven.

This writing is not about the maple tree as much as it is
about my prayer to God that day. The maple trees were simply
a pretty scene on a very pleasant day to pray. I have always
loved maple trees, especially the large one that was in our front
yard. It was majestic and beautiful, full of so much color during
changes of the seasons, particularly in the fall. These three small
maple trees were in our back yard, and I took a leaf from the
smallest one and glued it in my journal. Most of it has come off

the page through the years, but I was able to save a piece of it after thirty years!

Recollection of Deep Joy and Peace in a New Physical and Spiritual Life

October 4:

"I will praise the LORD all my life; I will sing praise to my God as long as I live" (Ps. 146:2).

Oh, powerful God, Father of healing any sickness, Maker of beauty and richness in the earth, I come before You with thanks in my heart and peace and security in my life. I reflect upon the last seven years not knowing that the incidents would dramatically shape and change my life. Oh, how difficult it was to have such deep depression, yet You changed my life by allowing me to walk with You and know Your love, forgiveness, and Your son, Jesus Christ. Lord, I thank you for taking such a dark and horrible time and giving me a new physical and spiritual life, one which will hopefully help other lives. In addition to helping me recover from the serious and deep depression in my senior year of high school, You later gave me the gift of salvation.

CHAPTER 16

I Want to Publish My Writings!

"Take delight in the LORD, and he will give you the desires of your heart" (Ps. 37:4).

November 15:

I believe that some of man's best work has been accomplished during great bursts of energy, the sky's the limit kind of feeling. The desire, and need to write a book was so strong, and I actually began seriously thinking about writing one during the summer of 1985, but I didn't think of actually publishing my writings. The following writings show my longing to do so:

> The time has come for me to share my love to people.
> I am full of energy and thanks to God for making
> My life a happy, healthier, and a secure one.

I believe if there is one person who needs to smile or needs to cry that I am ready and willing to help. With God's help, I want to show someone a new way, the right and only way. Help me Lord to do Your will.

Special Reflections and an Extraordinary Woman Used by God

December: What Is the Christmas Spirit?

I love the lights, the Christmas shows, movies, specials, and the Christmas carolers.
It warms my heart to be with friends and family and to go downtown, and have hot chocolate
After sled riding, and other times before Christmas. I like the baking and the festive
Scents I smell at the gift shops, and fireplaces and a little snow sparkling on the lawn.
All of these things mean so much to me at Christmas and give me a holiday spirit.
They are wonderful and fond memories, but I want to know what it means to have the true
Christmas spirit, not simply a holiday spirit. All of those things are nice, fun, and nostalgic,
yet the real Christmas spirit lies in Jesus, God's Son, who came here on that still night to change the lives of mankind. Give me that blessed Spirit, Lord—the real Christmas spirit that comes from only You.

I will always enjoy and appreciate, the holiday festivities, shows, movies, and being with my family. I believe most of us long for that during Christmas, but I desire to concentrate on the birth of Jesus Christ and have a balance between the holiday fun and His birth.

March 1986:

I met a very nice and kind lady named Lois at Gloria Marshalls. She has inspired me, and God, in his mysterious ways, has brought us together.

My book's guidelines: (1) Inspire and help people; (2) Double space for the manuscript; (3) Write about children, poems or writings about nature, people, and God; (4) I want to include pictures and will write about eternal life that you get when you trust and receive Jesus Christ into your life.

I saw Lois at Gloria Marshall's almost every day, so we got to know each other on a personal level. Soon after we met, she told me she was a published author and shared with me the books that she had published. I told her about my aspirations to publish my writings, and she gave me guidelines on how to accomplish that. She was so encouraging and told me what I should do.

I read both of her very inspiring and compelling books and was amazed in her deep faith, strength, and courage that she had in God. It's time for me to seriously consider taking the unknown challenge of writing a book. I suppose I have wanted to try this for many years, but now God is telling me to begin now. The energy and spiritual vitality are present, and as far as I'm concerned, it isn't a dream that can't come true or an unrealistic accomplishment because, with God, all is possible. If I really want to do this, I believe with all my heart that God is behind me every step of the way. Let me delight in the Lord for a gift that He has given to me.

At one point, I knew God was leading me every step of the way with my writings. Even back then, I pretended and dreamed of being an author. But I didn't actually think it would happen. I just always said, "I want to write a book!"

It has been a while since I have written about my daily routine or what is going on in my life. The Lord has certainly strengthened me during the last few weeks with depression and mood swings. I believe this because I have called upon Him during trying moments and, yes, there have been some. I now know, and am learning each day to accept the way God has made me.

"I praise you because I am fearfully and wonderfully made; your works are wonderful, I know that full well." Psalm 139:14

My book is coming along, if not on paper, then in my thoughts. When I see people I know or meet strangers, I then write about them. God has been showing me how to set priorities so I can serve him in everything I do. I could write forever, but I need to get my rest.

Thank you, God for loving me. Oh, Lord, what can I write before I go to sleep? I thank you for relaxing my body and slowing my mind down so that I may end this day with peace. You know, God, I am beginning to recognize the mood swings more quickly, and each day it seems like You show me how to deal with them better. But you see, work is tense for me at times. Lord, I am truly thankful for how you have sent people to me so I can help them. I really want to help change somebody's life if they are depressed, sad, or lonely. And You are the only one who can truly help and give hope to that person. Use me as an instrument. I must strive each day to live like You. Have me walk closely to You and Your Son, Jesus Christ.

My favorite way to express faith, feelings toward mankind, friends, and family is by writing in my journals. The biggest reason I want to do something with my writings is because of the energy and love for life that You have given to me. I have the deepest desire stemming from my heart to share with the world, my experiences, tribulations, and a joy and peace that lasts because of God and His Son, Jesus Christ.

It seems strange, Lord, but every bit of it is possible if You want me to be a published author. I thank you for helping me bring out the qualities of the fall season that I want to capture in my story. I believe and trust that You will show me more. This is the time I began writing a manuscript and in the introduction of it, I wrote, "It was fall time," and I saved the rough draft and put it in a folder with several other writings. Many years later, when I decided to publish, I used the original beginning of the story.

CHAPTER 17

Quiet Moments with God

I've been here at this park with a lake that is serene and beautiful before; at least it seems like I have. I saw the same things when I was here before, but now, I have a different mind, a new attitude about life. So, what is different? I will tell you. Before I had no peace, happiness, or a saving faith in Jesus Christ. Now I do, and what I see and hear is something that cannot be compared to anything else. For my heart is at peace, my mind at rest, and my soul is saved.

"May the God of hope fill you with all joy and peace as you trust in him, so that you may overflow with hope by the power of the Holy Spirit" (Rom. 15:13).

Peaceful Winter Snow and Waiting for God to Direct My Life

It is so peaceful in the midst of winter. Oh, if I were outside to enjoy it even more, I could see a squirrel lightly skipping over the clean snow and hear the snow fall as quiet as it might be. And even though my heart is longing for the freshness of spring, I still enjoy the peaceful, snowy, coziness of winter. I don't understand my life right now, but I'll be patient and wait upon You, Lord, to direct me.

There seems to be so many changes like how the seasons change, and my body is swaying me one way while my heart is going another. I don't believe I want to give up because I never have through any trial, but I'm just not happy where I am in my life. Before I believed in Jesus Christ, my goals and my desires were different, and I didn't have a joy that could last forever. Now God, I'm learning about what You want and my calling in life, and I believe You are leading me in a different direction than I'm walking now. So, Lord, please be with me, hold my hand, and walk with me through these indecisive moments. Let me listen to Your still voice, and I'll certainly give You the praise. Please, God, help me to live a pure and righteous life, resisting worldly temptations, and help me to focus on You. I look forward to spring and all of its beauty, freshness, and sunshine that you have created.

Gentle Spirit

It's morning, Lord; you have showered us with another
Beautiful snow that sparkles and sits so
perfectly on and in-between
The branches of the trees. I'm at peace,
Lord! You have given me such a joyful
And energetic spirit, and I know it comes
from no one but You.

Thank you for this time, God.
Thank you for Your gentle spirit for

It makes me be the kind of person I want to be,
who I need to be, for You.

Thank you, God, for the fresh morning
that I awoke to this morning.
I know you are slowly but wonderfully revealing Your
Fresh season of spring. Once again, the days will be longer
And children will still be playing until the last minute
of daylight.

You'll paint all the yards, parks, and gardens with beautiful
Colors of pink, yellow, blue, and so many more. Everyone's
Heart will be renewed—a rebirth just as spring symbolizes.
Thank you for this season and all of the seasons that You
Give, for it seems like we are always in the mood for them as
They unfold their beauty.

A Quiet Place with God

Everyone needs a special place
in which they can go and be alone
To pray, meditate, and feel the peace and presence of God.
A place that overflows with silence. A place to relieve your
Troubles and pressures from the day.
My place is out in the country where I hear nothing.
There are no cars, buses, or people's voices.
I found it at the perfect time when I was discouraged and in
need of a time of solitude with God.
There are hills and woods in this area

So that you can walk or ride your bike.
There are beautiful sounds of
Birds and dogs barking, but still a pleasant sound,
and very relaxing.
Thank you, God, for my special place.

A Quiet Place

There is a quiet place
Far from the rapid pace
Where God can soothe my troubled mind.
Sheltered by tree and flower
There in my quiet hour
With Him my cares are left behind.
Ralph Carmichael and The Young People, 1969

April 7:

Because your love is better than life, my lips will glorify
you. I will praise you as long as I live, and in your name,
I will lift up my hands" (Ps. 63:3–4)

I have been crucified with Christ and I no longer live,
but Christ lives in me. The life I now live in the body, I
live by faith in the Son of God, who loved me and gave
himself for me (Gal. 2:20)

I used to question what a man meant when he said he is
nothing without God. My life was not full of immorality and
corruption, but my heart was unhappy and always searching for

peace and joy. I needed something to stay in my life, something that the world cannot offer. One day I found everything that I needed, all that I was looking for.

Now, as I walk with Him, I realize how incomplete I am without Jesus in my heart and life.

I no longer wonder what a man means when he says he is nothing without God.

I know that without Him, my power to strive to be whatever He would have me to be is limited.

God gives me what I need to reach any goal. I'm able to persevere through the trials this life has, and appreciate every breath He gives to me. Then someday, I will be with Him in heaven in His glorious presence.

I am so glad that God loves me, am so grateful that He restores my heart and gently takes away my fears and gives me peace about my problems.

Making Progress on My Story

May 26:

I have one paragraph finished in my book. I feel good, but more important is if God is pleased, and I hope He is. Something good happened this afternoon. A good friend, Ed from high school, visited me. He is doing well, and we both had the chance to reminisce and just spend time together. We shared what was going on in our lives, and I read the introduction from my manuscript about fall and what it means to different people. I didn't actually tell him that I wanted to publish my writings, but he knew my passion about writing. I like how I'm writing about the seasons that God created compared to the seasons of our lives.

I want to listen to God speak to me through His Word. I'm able to appreciate each season He gives and every season of my life.

July 20:

"The LORD will give strength to his people; the LORD blesses his people with peace" (Ps. 29:11).

Oh, how my body felt physically and spiritually weak. Now, I have peace and rest since I gave my troubles to the Lord. I went bike riding and found a place of serenity in God's world of nature, with no people or cars, and I gave all of my doubts, fears, and burdens to the Lord.

I rode my bike on a country road, and as I went up the steep hills, I wasn't sure I knew where I was going. I just rode. There were no directions, but I simply trusted the Lord to lead me home. It's interesting how riding up and down the hills mimic how my life has been. Riding down the steep hills relieved me from the pressure and worry about my life. It was very exhilarating and rejuvenating.

A Sweet Southern Faith

July 21:

It's always nice to visit Mrs. Lucas because she has a lot of blessings to share with me about what "The good Lord" has done for her. She's one of these old-fashioned Southern Christians who has a lot of love and hospitality to give. I'm thankful that God still sends people like her our way, and especially my way. Mrs. Lucas was my neighbor who lived across the street. She prayed for me and had others pray after I was admitted to the hospital in 1977. Later, God heard her prayers and others who were praying for me, because as I wrote earlier, people were surprised about the progress I had been making. She knew how sick I was during that weekend in October of 1977. I'm pretty certain that my parents shared with her how I was doing during my stay in the hospital. It's strange to look back when I was fourteen and how I didn't know about salvation, but Mrs. Lucas did. I'm so thankful that years later, we were able to talk about God together, how she had prayed for me during that bizarre weekend, and even later into my early twenties. The best part was that she knew I had trusted Jesus as my Savior, so we always shared things about God together either on her front porch or inside of her home.

The Quiet Moments

September 23:

It's the quiet times that I so appreciate when I look out my bedroom window and see the leaves blowing on the beautiful maple tree. It's the quiet times that bring about a calmness from God that takes me away from the world and all of its troubles and changes. It's the quiet times that draw me closer to my Lord when I need His strength to know and rest in His Word. Thank you, Lord, for giving me this time to listen to Your gentle, reassuring voice that everything will be just fine. So often I would come home from work, school, or other places and look outside the window, stare at the tree, and relax during any time of the year. It was most beautiful in the fall. Years later on one particular visit to the home where I grew up, I noticed that the tree had been cut down. That was sad to me, but it was very old.

January 1, 1987:

The Snowy Pine Tree

Without much notice I glanced
At the snowy pine tree, that my wonderful God created.
So small and set apart to see, but full of life and
beauty for me.

It reminded me of how He has made each one of us. We
are small, yet when our heavenly Father lives within
our hearts
There exists an abundance of life full of radiance, love and
Beauty that openly shares itself to the world.

Oh Lord, make me like the little snowy pine tree
So small and set apart, but full of beauty for
The world to see.

I saw this pine tree after a large snowfall that we had in
Lancaster. It was so pretty and full, standing by itself. I enjoyed
the beauty of it so much that I took a picture of it. I wrote this
writing in calligraphy on parchment paper and in the back-
ground is a sketched picture of the tree. Then I wrote a letter to
Maria, a senior in high school who I knew at the church where
I attended. We worshipped at the same church, and I gave it
to her as a gift to show my gratitude toward the sweetness and
kindness that she and her family showed toward me.

CHAPTER 18

Struggling to
Keep My Moods Balanced

February 18, 1987:

Sometimes I feel like I am on a train that is running forever. My mind and body feel like a rollercoaster. I have been extremely wound up lately. I need a day of rest, preferably ten hours of nonstop sleep! I feel that not taking the lithium has made me really hyper. For the first time in a long time, I have felt anxious about my mood swings (More manic symptoms, not depressive ones). I experienced mood swings when I wasn't on my medication, as I wrote earlier in other journal entries. This particular time wasn't bad. I always just prayed and then would find relief. Still, at times, it was very difficult.

February 28:

I'm at Mom and Dad's house right now while they are in Kentucky, and I greatly appreciate this time of solitude that the Lord has given to me. For the last two months, my schedule has been very busy and surrounded by people. And now, after many days of teaching, loving, and disciplining kindergarteners and first graders, I need and desire quiet time to pray to God. The time spent was a blessing from God. He has shown me how children are and should be, and they have taught me more about love and appreciation for life. I love the Lord and all that He means to me, now and forever.

"One of those days, Jesus went out to a mountainside to pray and spent the night praying to God" (Luke 6:12).

The Young and Elderly Making a Positive Impact

March 1:

As I walked out the door to visit Pauline this morning, I forgot to take my purse. Later I broke my ceramic duck that Ann and I made in ceramics class. What a frustrating day! But I learned that God stands taller than my absent-minded ways, and I know He loves me even during those times when I don't like myself. During my visit with Pauline, I was able to tell her that each of us needs God before we can find true peace and joy. I told her that a form of religion gives you nothing, but a life with Jesus gives you everything. I'm so glad when God leads me in a conversation as I share the gospel and what He has done for me, and what He is able to for others. I felt lonely after church, but then one of my students, Rachel, gave me a sweet note, and a friend asked me out for pizza, which made me feel better. I should not let loneliness bother me because He is always with me. Rachel was a very sweet and kind little girl. One day I gave her a hug and said to her, "Someday I hope I have a little girl like you!"

I initially met Pauline when she was in her mid-seventies. When I worked at Gloria Marshalls, I became acquainted with her because she exercised there. We developed a unique friendship. She lived just a few blocks from my house on Spring Street. She was a lonely person who had family troubles and challenging health issues. We sat on her porch and talked a lot, and I visited her fairly often and remember feeling bad for her because of her tough family situation. We had these special and important times together for a couple of years. One day when I went to her home, her family informed me that her health had declined and she had to move into a nursing home. I knew she was struggling with physical and mental health issues, but was still sad and disappointed that she needed to move out of her home. I wasn't able to visit her anymore, but that evening, I wrote in my journal: I hope Pauline accepts Jesus Christ as her Lord and Savior, and knows how much God loves her.

March 17:

I had a wonderful day at school. As I walked into the classroom, I felt as if the Lord had given me a new attitude and a more enthusiastic heart toward my students, and they sensed my positivity. They're so sensitive. It seems like my attitude or mood has an effect on their mood and day. I babysat Kelli, my niece, today and sang songs to her about Jesus and God. I love her so much and am hoping Jan and Mark will trust the Lord, so one day Kelli, too, may believe in and receive Jesus Christ as her Savior. I'm very thankful for the special bond that Kelli and I have.

Restoration, Slowing Down

"Seek the LORD while he may be found, call on him while he is near" (Isa. 55:6)."In peace I will lie down and sleep, for you alone, LORD, make me dwell in safety"(Ps. 4:8).

April 16:

I must say I have had a wonderful and relaxing vacation here in Florida. I experienced joy and peace. Since mid-December, my life has been going too fast, swirling round and round, like a person riding a merry-go-round that is never going to stop! I need the Lord's help in slowing down, getting adequate rest, and eating properly.

I went to Florida with my parents during spring break. During that time, we visited Barb and Jayne, and it was fun and relaxing. I slept well and had time to spend with God. I thought about my unusually busy schedule the last six months and how it drained me. I was teaching kindergarteners and first graders, tutoring a couple of students, babysitting, and working at the fitness salon part time.

An Answer to a Long-Awaited Prayer

"You may ask me for anything in my name, and I will do it" (John 14:14).

May 9:

I am more productive because I have slowed down and gotten adequate rest. I love the Lord for giving that to me. The best thing He has done is answer my prayer that Dad would go to church with me. One night back in April, I felt a heavy burden for my father and really cried out to God to show His power in my dad's life. I reflected back to the last ten years of our family's troubles, the onset of bipolar disorder, and later the deep and very serious state of depression, our fun family vacations, and other life situations. But in all honesty the last ten years were hard on my parents and, at times, my sister and brother. I'm so glad, and thankful that he came to church with me.

CHAPTER 19

Is God Calling Me to Help People Who Have Depression?

July 1:

*W*ell, I have started a writing area. It will be downstairs, and I will use the desk, which is Dad's really nice old one. I tried doing this a couple of years ago but wasn't consistent. My day at work was a blessed one. Tina and I worked together, and she knows I'm a Christian. Teresa and I talked about the seasons and how God puts us in the mood for each one of them. However, the best blessing from God came at 3:00 this afternoon. I saw the 3–11 shift nurse at the nursing home where I work, and she told me that she felt depressed. Well, we talked a little bit, but the blessing came when I told her how I had been at Riverside Hospital in ninth grade and how the Lord helped me with my depression. The Lord gave me the courage to continue telling her how I came to know and receive Jesus Christ. The entire day was very good. After church last night, I shared with Barbara about my journaling and desire to write for God, and she encouraged me by saying perhaps this is what God wants me to do. We prayed about it together, but the most special blessing was how I felt a close bond with her. Barbara and her family meant so much to me because they loved the Lord and showed genuine Christian love to me.

August 14:

"The LORD will watch over your coming and going both now and forever more" (Ps. 121:8).

"Though my mother and father forsake me, the Lord will receive me" (Ps. 27:10).

It has been a difficult time between me and my parents. Tuesday evening, I began feeling quite frustrated and very upset. It was if I had so much inside of me, and it was all I could do from breaking down into tears. I love them more than I ever have, but it can never be the same because I am not the same person. So, that evening, I left to take a walk to find peace and communion with the Lord. Though it was a beautiful evening and I knew of God's deep love for me, I still felt tense, and alone but ready to give the anxiety, frustration, and questions to Him. I thought about my work at the nursing home and how that summer job would soon end. I reflected upon my Christian experience, church, and all of my wonderful friends there. I came home as dark was approaching and sat still on the bank in our front yard. I looked at our maple tree that really feels like my own personal tree. Peace began to fill my mind, body, and soul. Then, it's as if God spoke to me, and said You are my child and Jesus my Son lives in your heart. And even though it's difficult at times, I find I can be removed from my parents but still love them.

I felt better and soon thereafter went to bed and continued to pray to God. I'm reminded of how grateful I am and glad to write what He has done in my life. He reassured me that He truly does watch over my coming and going through this journey. God has given me more strength and appreciation for who I am in Him, and the rich and completely satisfying life that I have. My parents didn't like it when I began going to a different church. I was very active in the church where my family attended. I was in choir and children ministries, and I loved being involved in them. When I started going to a different church and later trusting Jesus Christ as my Savior, many changes happened in my life. My parents, particularly my mother, struggled with me attending another church. For several years I felt separated from them, but later I knew in my heart that they loved me.

Psalm 121

I lift up my eyes to the mountains, where does my help come from?
My help comes from the LORD, the maker of heaven and earth.
He will not let your foot slip, he who watches over you will not slumber; indeed, he who watches Israel will neither slumber nor sleep.
The LORD watches over you, the LORD is your shade at your right hand; the sun will not harm you by day, nor the moon by night. The LORD will keep you from all harm, he will watch over your life, the LORD will watch over your coming and going, both now and forevermore.

This was the first time I read Psalm 121 when I took that walk and prayed and talked to God. What a powerful and beautiful description of how I was feeling and experiencing my life during that time. Today, there are moments I meditate on that particular Psalm.

CHAPTER 20

Appreciating the Four Seasons;
Challenging Times of Life

October 12:

$\mathcal{F}$all is here and that means colorful leaves and blue fresh skies. Of course, it wouldn't be fall without the cooler evenings, bright orange pumpkins sitting on the neighbor's porches, and apples on the trees. I really like this season. It's my very favorite one that God created. I enjoy and appreciate the vibrant colors of red, orange, and yellow. Actually, all of the seasons are special to me since the deep depression is gone, and since I've trusted Jesus Christ as my Savior. I now enjoy my life so much and genuinely appreciate it to the fullest. I believe God has given me a true seed of love to stay in my heart forever and hopefully share it to others throughout my entire life. It is because of God who made the heavens and earth that I am able to appreciate each season He created and the seasons of my life. Throughout my journals I wrote several writings about the four seasons and compared them with seasons I experienced in my life.

Timeless One

Chorus: You are Alpha Omega, Lord of all. Every season is guided by your hand.

From beginning to ending you are God dust to dust we will trust you timeless one. Phillip Keveren Chorus And Orchestra, 2013

CHAPTER 21

A *Frightening Stretch of Moderate Depression*

Truly my soul finds rest in God; my salvation comes from him. Truly he is my rock and my salvation; and he is my fortress, I will never be shaken. (Ps. 62:1–2).

The righteous cry out, and the LORD hears them; he delivers them from all their troubles; The LORD is close to the broken hearted and saves those who are crushed in spirit. (Ps. 34:17–18).

But you oh LORD, are a shield around me, my glory, the One who lifts my head high. I call out to the LORD, and he answers me from his holy mountain. (Ps. 3:3–4).

October 17:

I never thought I would experience the same level of depression as I did in 1981, and I'm definitely not now. Thank God I am only having mild symptoms of it, but it really scares me. Lord, I will do my best to endure this time for I know in time it will pass. I promise to keep hope and trust in You and not lose sight of the golden streets of glory that await for me some day. I will not waste my time and energy on pleading to You, and asking, why me, God? I want to thank You and know You are carrying me always. I promise to not resort to unnatural forms of healing but to do what You would have me to do.

I don't remember why I was having moderate depression, or what triggered it, but I was. "Unnatural forms of healing" simply meant one thing: that I didn't want to start taking the lithium again. I still believed that God could help and even heal me, and I didn't want to take my medication.

Hope and Peace Restored

"Because of the LORD's great love we are not consumed, for His compassions never fail. They are new every morning, great is your faithfulness" (Lam. 3:22–23).

October 18:

In answer to my heartfelt prayer, the Lord certainly blessed me as I read a powerful Bible passage before I went to bed last night. He really increased my faith and reassured me that He is in control. I woke up this morning feeling better, less depressed, and free of stress and confusion. The B vitamin may have helped but did not completely take care of the problem. My wonderful God helped me and I'm ready to tell a person in need of His amazing grace. I love the Lord.

November 1:

"You will keep in perfect peace those whose minds are steadfast because they trust in you. Trust in the LORD forever, for the LORD himself is the rock eternal" (Isa. 26:3–4).

There is such a strong peace in my heart that comes only from God. I suppose it's worth all of the praying, walking, and crying I've been doing lately. And yet, as I think of Jesus and what He endured on the cross and His great suffering, I feel uncomfortable to worry or fret about anything! Still, I know that God is so caring and powerful in my life and other lives as well, and He cares about every detail of our lives. When I trust in Him and allow Him to carry me through times of loneliness, frustration, and confusion, I'm assured that there is no problem too big for Him. I'm glad and thankful to not only say that but believe it and know it. Thank you God for being my peace.

Jesus Is My Peace

Jesus is the peace that I have found
Jesus, he's the one who makes me sound
Through all that I endure,
Every place where I may go,
This I know, He is my peace.
Jesus is the joy that's in my heart.
Jesus is the one who does the part
In turning all the sorrows into sunshine for tomorrow.
He's the joy that's in my heart.
Chorus:
He's the one who gives us life fresh and always new.

He's the one who makes us laugh and cry, but we still want to try.

And he's the man who died on the cross can't you see for you and me, to give us a life of peace. Jesus is the peace that we can find.

"Jesus Is My Peace" is one of the songs I wrote. I wrote the lyrics and melody, and my friend, Marla arranged the music and accompanied me on the piano. She had a natural gift and played beautifully.

CHAPTER 22

Memorable and Special People During Christmas; Poignant Reflection

"Therefore the Lord himself will give you a sign: The virgin will conceive and give birth to a son, and will call him Immanuel" (Isa. 7:14).

December 25:

*W*ell, it's over. Christmas day has passed for another year, but my desire is to have Him in my heart throughout the entire year. Last night in my restless sleep, I thought of how the people many years ago were waiting for the Messiah. It's amazing and almost impossible to comprehend that time period in history. Then, at 11:45, I heard someone knock at the door. Mom answered, and someone said, "This is for Robin; it's not much." Her voice was pleasant, but I was half asleep so I couldn't make out who the person was. Mom told me it was my friend, Cyndi. That made me really think about our friendship, and my love and appreciation for her. God has really blessed two people who want to serve God and others. Again, I'm thankful for his love, peace, and hope that He gives to me. Cyndi and I met at church and became friends. Later, we worked together at Fairfield Christian Academy.

December 27:

I'm staying at Donna's house and helping her mother-in-law, Catherine, for three days. Catherine, who has dementia, is a kind woman and I was thankful and glad I could assist with her early morning routine. It was a good thing because God allowed me to be a blessing to her, and she was a blessing to me! As Catherine left the next morning, I thought about her as the driver of the van transported her, along with the other folks, to the senior care activity center. In spite of Catherine's limitations and problems with her dementia, there is human pride within her and a mark of strength and stamina that refuses to let her become discouraged.

The Lord taught me how important it is to look around at others who are hurting and know that I'm not the only person who has experienced suffering. Catherine was a woman I helped, who lived with her son and his wife and children. I had no idea at the time that several years later, I would be working with people who had dementia, particularly ones with Alzheimer's disease. In 1990, I received my certified nurse assistant's license and since then have devoted my work to caring for and working with seniors. I'm thankful to God to have worked in various units, or areas, such as skilled nursing, assisted living, life enrichment (coordinating activities for seniors), memory care, and rehabilitation. Throughout my journaling, I wrote various writings about my elderly friends. My life has been so enriched, and I am incredibly thankful and blessed to be a positive influence in their lives as they have been in mine.

A Poignant Reflection

Today, I reflect back to spring of 1976 when I was thirteen years old. I began experiencing unhealthy mood swings even for a teenager. They were more depressive ones than manic episodes. I was so down that I went to the assistant principal who I liked and said to him, "What do you do when you're very depressed? He talked to me, and I listened, but I didn't say much.

He called my parents, and my mom had me stay home the next day. She said, "You just needed a day off from school." She or my dad had no idea that less than six months later I would be hospitalized and diagnosed with a mood disorder.

I wrote the following journal entry in the spring of 1976:

I went to Lancaster High School with Jan, and I was shocked to see how big and overwhelming the school was which made my troubles in eighth grade seem so trivial. Furthermore, I sometimes dwell on my problems. Later, in the fall of 1977 when I was in the hospital, my doctor told me something which I will not forget: "The worst thing you can do when you have a problem is sit around and think on it or worry about it." How true. I need to go out and use my energy to help someone else so my troubles will flee away like dandelion seeds being blown into an open field. Poof!

If I have learned anything, it is this: I should never be depressed because there isn't time to spend on my problems or little weaknesses. There is an entire world out there full of people who need love, salvation, and peace that comes only from God through His Son, Jesus Christ. I have those things, and I'm thankful to live in a country that is free. I will therefore forget about myself and look at others who need to be told and shown this marvelous gift called salvation that is given to the richest, the poorest, the proud one, the strong-willed one, and the "perfect" one. I know because He gave it to me! "Give thanks in all circumstances, for this is God's will for you in Christ Jesus" (1 Thess. 5:18).

CHAPTER 23

Much joy; In His Time

January 12, 1988:

This evening, when I got home from work and checked the mail I noticed that I got a card from Emi. I cried out of joy as I read her lovely card, accompanied by a letter. The Lord works mysteriously. I prayed Wednesday evening about being lonely, but God took my sadness away, and I felt at peace because God's love was protecting me. The letter and card from her made my evening. It really lifted my spirits and lessened the loneliness. I'm anxious about my dating life, but I know I need to give this situation to God. Peace came over me, as Emi greatly encouraged me in saying, trust the Lord, and don't be anxious. Thank you, Lord, for my wonderful friend Emi. I love her and ask You to bless her with Your love and strength, whatever she needs today. Thank you for helping me in giving problems to You, and I know in time, a special male friend will come my way. Emi, a student who I knew in high school and later became very close friends with at Ohio University's branch in Lancaster. She played the piano, and I sang, as we performed at a couple of variety shows in college. We spent many hours at her home playing and singing Amy Grant songs. I have many fond memories of spending time with her lovely and gracious parents and sister, Ginny, and brother, Thomas.

January 15:

This evening, we had our end-of-the-school-year program at Fairfield Christian Academy. My students were so proud to be finishing school and advancing to the next grade. The guest speaker, Kevin, was quite good, and I had a chance to meet him after the program, and we talked briefly. It must have been a strain on him during those times of Abbie's illness. Abbie, Kevin's wife, died within the last year, leaving behind him and two children, Sarah and Ryen, ages seven and five.

January 16:

This day has been very wonderful and unusual. This morning about 8:00, Arlene and Dan, friends of mine and sister-in law and brother-in-law to Kevin who spoke at the school program, invited me over to their home for breakfast. Then she wondered if Kevin and I could go to the youth rally. Since he lived out of town, he spent that evening at Arlene and Dan's home. I accepted the invitation, and had a light breakfast. Kevin asked me to show him Rising Park, a beautiful and very well-loved park in Lancaster that has a mountain, Mount Pleasant. It was a sunny winter morning, and we had an enjoyable time. Later that evening, he went to the youth rally at church and is coming back next Sunday to attend church with me. I prayed and trusted God to send me a special friend, but I really didn't expect it to be this soon. With Emi's letter and my faith regarding dating,

God is working! How, I don't know, but I'm amazed at His wonderful ways, and most of all the way He brings people together.

February 10:

I had a long and peaceful walk and sat by the creek which is so quietly hidden from the world and asked the Lord's direction for me and Kevin. If God would have it, I would like to marry him some day. I'm praying for God to direct our lives and intervene if we should not be together. I think of his children, Sarah and Ryen, for I want to be a good mother to them.

Chapter 24

A Perplexing Setback

March 16:

I'm going through a depression. I don't think it's because of stress from my classes in college because those are going pretty well. I want to start going to church on Wednesdays again. I miss the services, and I need to get out of this dark time or rut that I'm experiencing.

"Listen to my prayer, oh God, do not ignore my plea; hear me, and answer me" (Ps. 55:1-2).

Do I Need My Medication?

God is wonderful! I was feeling down and spent time in prayer, walked into the classroom, and had a new and positive outlook. Wednesday afternoon, Kevin surprised me and drove to Lancaster. We went to the mid-week service at church. We each gave testimonies, thanking God for His goodness to us. Things are looking up for me. I have been walking and appreciating the snowy, sunny mornings, and I haven't been depressed.

"I love the LORD for He heard my voice; he heard my cry for mercy. Because he turned his ear to me, I will call on him as long as I live" (Ps. 116:1–2). This Bible verse is and always will be one of my favorite verses. I had seriously thought about taking lithium again, but I really don't want to. I just became afraid, that's all, and that feeling is terrible! After work, I took another walk and stopped at one point to cry out of joy, thanking God for touching me by relieving the depression. Soon, it will be spring break, and I am going to meet Kevin's parents who live in Michigan. I'm looking forward to it.

Spring Vacation

March 27:

Kevin, Sarah, Ryen and I are on our way to Holland, Michigan. God has lifted the mild depression I was experiencing. Walking and riding my bike has helped a lot, and we plan to walk during the visit in Holland.

March 29:

It's raining and chilly, but so far this trip has been really nice. Kevin's parents, Larry and Norie, are wonderful and kind. Kevin and I took a walk yesterday in the dunes where the fir trees are beautiful, majestic, and peaceful. God has really blessed me by bringing Kevin into my life. We have actually talked about the possibility of getting married. To some people it might seem quite soon, but when the Lord works, He works! He knows what Sarah and Ryen need, and it is an honor to think that God might choose me to be the mother of these children and the wife of Kevin. God, continue to please lead our paths.

March 30:

Last night was the best evening of my life. During the day, Kevin and I spoke about engagement and he told me, "You decide on the wedding day, and I'll decide on the engagement time."

"Fine," I jokingly said. "How about tonight?"

"Right, he said, I don't even have the ring!"

We had dinner in the early evening, and as we sat down, the server brought me a card. It had two boats on it and was very pretty. It said: "Two boats on separate journeys to the same place, may we go together?" Then Kevin wrote: "Will you marry me? I love you, Robin."

I was shocked but eagerly replied, "Yes!"

Then he presented me with a beautiful ring. He certainly surprised me as he intended on doing. I love him and am actually engaged to be married! I am quite thankful for our relationship. I love the Lord.

The Right Decision

April 16:

Well, I am taking the lithium again and am slightly confused about deciding to do so since I was determined not to take it. I wanted to trust in God alone to help me manage the mood swings and depression. Kevin helped me to sort my thoughts about the subject, and he told me that God made the medication and that it's okay to take it. He also said that God honored the fact that I trusted in Him during the years that I didn't take it. Meanwhile, I'll be patient and wait to see what happens.

April 19:

This period of depression has ended. I felt fine again within a few days. Lithium is a charm if it works, as a doctor told me years later. At that time, it was wise to resume taking it.

April 24:

I've accepted the fact that I am taking my medicine again, but it has been an adjustment. For the past three years, I have not taken it, and I believed in my heart that God had healed me and that it would be wrong to ever take it again. I have learned, however, that I need it and that it's okay to take medicine. I haven't and do not want to ever experience that deep, hopeless state of depression again. I believe that will never happen again. I just always wanted to trust God to help me with mood swings, particularly with the depressive side, and he did. He still does because He can't change. His faithfulness is amazing, and His promises are so true. "God did this so that, by two unchangeable things in which it is impossible for God to lie, we who have fled to take hold of the hope set before us may be greatly encouraged." (Heb. 6:18).

Chapter 25

Marriage and Two Very Special Children

*K*evin and I got married on July 23 in Lancaster at the First Presbyterian Church. We met January 15. He proposed to me two and a half months later, and we got married four months later. The story of how we met, my prayer to meet a friend, Emi's kind and sweet note, and my love for children created a perfect story. I prayed earnestly for God's will to be done in my life and Kevin's life, and for Sarah and Ryen's lives.

There were a few moments when I doubted or questioned getting married so quickly but I could not trust and listen to my instincts. In many ways, I was an emotional mess when it came to intimate relationships, but back then I didn't understand that. I really believed that Kevin could make my life complete, share my faith in the Lord, and eventually we would have children together.

Years later, I discovered the power and beauty of God's grace, faithfulness, forgiveness, and redemption. The events that later occurred are unbelievable, but God's amazing grace and redemption are powerful and extraordinary!

Welcoming Two Blessings into Our World

February 1990:

Michael Thomas, our little blessing, was born February 16, 1990, at 3:57 in the morning. He weighed seven pounds ten ounces, twenty inches long, and is simply beautiful! We are so thankful to have a precious and healthy baby boy with dark brown hair. The first miracle was to see this little creation enter into the world. Then the moment came when the doctor handed him to me and sweetly asked, "How would you like a boy?" Immediately Michael put his tiny hands in his mouth and around the blanket. My labor and delivery were pretty uneventful without any complications, for which I am thankful. He's special, and he is our baby to hold, to hug, and see grow and gradually familiarize himself to the world that God has created. Sarah and Ryen have been waiting for the birth of their first half-brother. Now they have one!

April 1990:

The joy I feel in my heart is almost impossible to express or explain. I am enjoying each waking moment of Michael's beautiful young life. His tiny hands are so warm as they grasp my finger or wrist as I feed him. His little, but strong, angelic body stretches so cutely in the mornings that you simply want to hold him closely to your chest. Then when he suddenly cries out of his deep sleep, it's so rewarding to rush back to his room and hold and comfort him. As a family, we are beginning to see his personality show. He is smiling, and I love calling the grandparents to tell them about the changes we see. He is our little bundle of joy!

March, 1991:

On March 23, 1991, God gave us a sweet and beautiful girl. We named her Kate Lynn, but we are calling her Katie. She weighed almost the same as Michael, seven pounds seven ounces and almost the same height as Michael, nineteen and three-quarter inches. She has very dark hair, almost black, and lots of it. I am so delighted to have a girl. Now, we have a boy and a girl and are very thankful to have these blessings.

For you created my inmost being, you knit me together in my mother's womb,

> I praise you because I am fearfully and wonderfully made;
> Your works are wonderful, I know that full well.
> My frame was not hidden from you when I was made in the secret place, when I was woven together in the depths of the earth. Your eyes saw my unformed body; all the days ordained for me were written in your book before one of them came to be. (Ps. 139:13–16)

April 1991:

Not writing in a journal for ten months about my thoughts and things happening in my life causes me to be a little "rusty." I want to write again and write more consistently. It always has and always will help me express my thoughts about people and events.

Children, a Special and Needed Blessing to My Elderly Friends

During my maternity leave, I took Katie to Raybrook Manor where I work and showed her off to some of the residents. She was only six weeks old, and everyone who saw her was so thrilled to see this beautiful tiny baby. I was so proud! I often took Michael and Katie to Raybrook Manor where I received my certification as a nursing assistant in Grand Rapids, Michigan. The residents always loved seeing them, for children are such a joy and blessing to older people. Later, as teenagers, when they needed to volunteer in a service program through school, they came to work with me and helped the residents with their activities.

CHAPTER 26

A Frightening and Shocking Truth

June 1992:

Shortly after the summer began in 1992, I began to realize that Kevin had a serious drinking problem. I remember going to bed at night, saying and then repeating to myself, "I married an alcoholic." I couldn't believe it, but the reality that my husband and the father of my children was one was extremely startling. Michael and Katie were toddlers, and Sarah and Ryen were eleven and ten. There were very few journal entries written in 1992 because a part of me was in denial, and part of me was busy being a mother to four children of great age differences. Life was simply too difficult and busy to journal. I didn't write much because it was the beginning of an incredibly difficult journey that Sarah, Ryen, Michael, Katie and I would unfortunately experience together for several years.

In 1996, I remember looking out the window one day and earnestly thinking to myself and saying to God that I wished I had the kind of faith I had when I was teaching at Fairfield Christian Academy in the mid-eighties. Back then before going to work, I would wake up early to read the Bible, pray, and have a quiet time talking to the Lord. As I stared out the window at the scenery, which was very pretty, I longed to have those moments again. God definitely increased my faith and gave me time to read the Word but not without immense pain, and grief.

Sadly, and tragically, my marriage ended in 1997. Because my book is not about divorce, I chose not to go into deep detail about it but rather concentrate on the powerful love and faithful support I got from my family, close friends, and so many people from my church. Above all, I am beyond thankful for God's amazing love, grace, forgiveness, and hope that I found during the journey and the process of healing. The healing season did not happen overnight. The following entries describe the pain yet also the peace that I experienced during a very dark and uncertain time before and after the divorce.

Seeing Beauty in the Midst of Pain

"The heavens declare the glory of God; the skies proclaim the work of his hands." (Psalm 19:1).

"So do not fear, for I am with you; do not be dismayed, for I am your God. I will strengthen you and help you; I will uphold you with my righteous hand" (Isa. 41:10).

November 10, 1996:

My heart is praising my Lord and Savior Jesus Christ! It snowed four to six inches last night, and it's simply breathtaking! Only God, the Creator of this world, could make a masterpiece of beauty such as what I am seeing this morning. The snow rests on each branch in a perfect manner, so that when you look at the entire tree, the white branches spread out so full, and majestic. I am not worshipping the tree but am amazed at God's creation. I see this morning God's handiwork in designing our first snowfall of the season and my son looking out the window in wonder. He enjoys looking at the trees. I told him when he was looking to think about God and just relax.

Oh Lord, I have felt this peace before and Your amazing love to me, but what's happening? I'm going through a lot of pain in my life like an emotional rollercoaster of many feelings and events that cause great anxiety. Yet there is a sense of calmness that allows me to release this season in my life to You. Only You, God, can give this gift of peace and assurance in the midst of such uncertainty. You are my strength. As the beautiful snow covers the dying fall leaves, Your powerful love covers my pain and will restore me to life and wholeness.

December 2:

"As the deer pants for streams of water, so my soul pants for you, my God. My soul thirsts for God, for the living God. When can I go and meet with God? My tears have been my food day and night" (Ps. 42:1–3).

Deliver me, oh Lord, from the anxious thoughts that I wrestle with. I long to read your Word and absorb it closely to my heart so that I will be changed, illuminated, and free from this mental anguish. Your many blessings given to me are mighty in number and rich in greatness. Clear my mind and help me to focus on You and the Word that is medicine to my body and strength to my soul. I need to be in the Word every day and in prayer with my Lord. I have been reading and talking to God about six days a week for the last couple of months.

My faith has increased, and I am gaining more strength and closeness to God. I am enjoying my Bible reading immensely and have read a lot of the Old Testament and most of the New Testament. I must admit I need God and His Word to help me with anger, hurt, and anxiety. Reading scripture helps me to be more like God and less like myself.

"Your word is a lamp for my feet, a light on my path" (Ps. 119:105).

CHAPTER 27

Deep Waters

"He heals the broken hearted and binds up their wounds" (Ps. 147:3).

April 20, 1997:

*M*uch time has passed, and much has happened. As I wrote earlier in the year, my heart felt broken. I have learned that your heart may break for a season, but God can mend it and heal the pain in His timing. Perhaps you just get a stronger heart that grows closer to Him as you daily give up the pain, disappointment, and anger. On a summer morning in 2019, while driving home from church, I listened to a song, and it deeply spoke to me. I asked God to show me a way to depict that broken season of my life, and He did. It wasn't that I was sad about my marriage ending because I had begun grieving years before about the loss of the relationship and hopes I had in having a complete home and family. It was more the ugliness, pain, suffering, and the immense collateral damage that occurred.

I highly encourage anyone who has a broken heart, or anyone who has had one, to take a moment to listen closely to this song. As I said on April 20, 1997: "I have learned that your heart may break for a season, but God can mend it." He mended mine.

> Tell your heart to beat again close your eyes and breath it in
> Let the shadows fall away
> Step into the light of grace
> Yesterday's a closing door
> You don't live there anymore
> Say goodbye to where you've been
> And tell your heart to beat again.
> Danny Gokey, Tell Your Heart to Beat Again, 2016

Challenging and Wearisome Times in Parenting

> When you pass through the waters, I will be with you; and when you pass through the rivers, they will not sweep over you. When you walk through the fire, you will not be burned; The flames will not set you ablaze." (Isaiah 43: 1-2).

July 11, 1998:
It has been exceedingly difficult lately because of a new parenting schedule with Michael and Katie's father, but I'm thankful to say we've had a fun summer. We went camping for the first time, which was an enjoyable experience, and we went to Michigan's Adventure which was very fun. We also have plans to to go to a baseball game, a water park in Battle Creek, and another camping trip. Most of all, it has been particularly good to see the children laugh, play, and simply be happy.

Sometimes the memories of the painful, ugly, and tragic events of the divorce and ensuing custody battle are overwhelming to me, but God is faithful as He hears me cry out to him in despair, and sometimes fatigue. Still, He continues to restore my strength and gives me peace and joy in the morning. I am thankful because I am becoming a stronger Christian who is more willing to serve him more effectively.

A Refreshing Outlook on Work, Parenting, and Special Friendships

June 14, 1999:

The Lord heard my prayers, needs and concerns about parenting. I prayed earnestly to the Lord, seeking His will and desiring to be obedient to Him. Peace and strength followed my prayer. Though at times loneliness comes over me, I turn to God, knowing He is always with me.

"The LORD himself goes before you and will be with you; he will never leave you nor forsake you. Do not be afraid; do not be discouraged" (Deut. 31:8).

Summer 2000:

I met Brenda when I worked at Park Village Pines in the memory care center. For a brief time, I worked as a certified nurse assistant, but later worked in the activities department, coordinating the activities for the residents. Brenda was an LPN and currently is today. We have love and compassion for people who suffer with dementia.

Shortly after we met, I learned that she was a Christian, which was encouraging for both of us. During that time, we were going through similar struggles of being single parents, so we understood each other's experiences. In 2013, she gave me a journal in which I wrote several writings. The front of it said: "For we live by faith not by sight" (2 Cor. 5:7). We have shared a lot of good times, creating good memories through the years, but also have gone through some difficult times together, and individually. When my dad was diagnosed with cancer, I was an emotional mess, and she was incredibly helpful and compassionate. She has experienced but has recovered from some serious health issues, and I'm thankful to have been there for her during those challenging and frightening times. I'm grateful for her faithfulness to me as a very loyal friend.

> I love you LORD, my strength. The LORD is my rock, my fortress, and my deliverer; my God is my rock, in whom I take refuge, my shield and the horn of my salvation, my stronghold. (Ps. 18:1–2).

> Therefore, He is also able to save completely those who come to God through him, because he always lives to intercede for them. (Heb. 7:25)

Tricia and I met in my mid-thirties at a community group activity that she invited me to through her church. It is at that event where we became friends. Later, we met for lunch, and she shared with me that she had bipolar disorder. I was so glad to meet someone that was a Christian and who understood my experience with a mood disorder that many people don't fully understand. We could easily identify with each other's experiences. She has an unwavering faith and joy in the Lord and never stops praying through the trials this life brings. She still laughs and rejoices over miracles she sees in her life and her children and husband's lives. I'm thankful for our friendship and enjoy our times as we have meals, share special and important conversations while taking walks, laughing, and praying together.

"Perfume, and incense bring joy to the heart, and the pleasantness of a friend springs from their heartfelt advice" (Prov. 27:9).

Val and I met in the late 90's. I was facilitating a small group called Coping with Divorce. I had attended this group to help me adjust to divorce. After I completed my sessions I had an opportunity to facilitate a group. Val who was experiencing divorce, attended the group and we became close friends. We have many things in common like theater, taking walks, meeting in coffee shops, and sharing stories about our lives and children's lives.

The best part about our friendship is how we have grown together in our faith in God through many years of joy, life's experiences, and loss of loved ones. I'll always remember the day I shared with her my plan to publish my writings. We were at a coffee shop, and I gave her a crash course on my dream to help others through my journal writings, and she was enthusiastic in my aspiration to publish my writings. She is very creative and enjoys making scrapbooks for her grandchildren and cards for her friends and family. When I look at the collage of pictures that she helped me make as a gift for my dad, I smile and am so grateful for her trustworthy friendship.

CHAPTER 28

Busy teenagers,
an Interruption in Journaling

January 3, 2003:

I began thinking that I was not going to write again, though I knew in my heart that I could never really quit writing. Journaling has helped me to express myself, write about others, and learn about and draw closer to God.

I had an interruption back in November 1999 with journaling because life in general was busy, stressful but also exciting. Much of my time I was focusing on Michael and Katie's lives, for they were teenagers, and busy with friends, school, sports, and church activities. My job was going well, and I loved what I was doing. I was still working at Park Village Pines but not as a Certified Nurse Assistant. I worked as a life enrichment coordinator, planning and leading events and activities for the senior residents.

A New Relationship

February 2004:

I met someone, and his name is Steve. He is kind and has a good sense of humor. We have been doing many things together and are currently in a Bible study. We talk about life with its frustrations, joys, and concerns. He makes me laugh, and we laugh a lot together. I dated after divorce, but most of those whom I dated did not share my Christian faith. Also, if I were to remarry, I had to think about Michael and Katie, regarding a stepfather. I believed that if I met someone and remarried, that would be fine, but if not, I was content in being single. I was comfortable and strong in my faith in the Lord, confident in my work and in parenting. I trusted God's plan for me whether that meant remarriage or remaining single.

A Sweet and Relaxing Time, Will I Publish Some Day?

July 10:

I'm at Katie's softball tournament in Jackson, Michigan. It's a wonderful park that has a very pretty and clear lake. There are boats and quaint homes around this lake and picnic areas where people are having cookouts. I'm away from responsibilities at home work, or just plain life that can sometimes overwhelm me. I'm watching the games and enjoying them. I'm thinking of solitude right now, something I have not experienced in a while. One reason is because I have chosen to not have it. Another reason is the kids' bodies are changing with adolescence, so I feel tense at times. I have seriously been contemplating resuming journaling again more consistently. It has always been so powerful in my life as I've expressed my feelings about how the Lord has blessed me during moments of adversity. I have had many ideas lately about organizing my writings and making a devotional or some kind of book to tell others how amazing God's grace is.

Steve and I are still seeing each other. We are compatible and have many of the same interests. We attend art shows and enjoy the theater, like taking walks, and going to sporting events. It hasn't been all fun and games as we have differences and are doing our best in communicating those differences with honesty and respect toward one another. The best and most important part is that our faith in the Lord is growing as we learn more about the Bible.

CHAPTER 29

Heartfelt Letters, Writings, and Remarriage

*T*he following letters I saved through the years and had no idea at the time that I would include them in my book. When I went through them several years later, I became very emotional but am grateful that the grief has turned into a peace and assurance of how the Lord worked in Michael and Katie's lives.

"And we know that in all things God works for the good of those who love him, who have been called according to his purpose" (Rom. 8:28).

2004:

Dear Katie,

I am writing you a letter for a couple of reasons. One being in response to your note that you gave to me about three weeks ago. The second reason is because I wanted to tell you a few things and tell you how much I love and care about you. Your note was kind and direct, and it was so good to hear you say that you appreciate the things I do for you. I especially like how you said that through the tough times, I have been there for you. The divorce is painful, I know. You were five years old, and your dad and I had just separated, and we were living in the apartment. It was Michael's birthday, and we had his party at McDonald's. Do you remember? Later that evening, you were sitting on my lap, and you said to me, "Mommy, I don't want Daddy to be mean, but I don't want a divorce." Then sometime later after your sixth birthday, you said, "Mommy, I want things to be normal again." I want Daddy to be the pastor, and I want to see Sarah and Ryen." You expressed your feelings so well. Your world as you knew it had turned upside down. Though God was always with us and you had a great Christian school with good friends, life was difficult and painful. It still is, at times; I understand.

Do you remember when I sang that song to you and Michael that had a verse in the Psalms? "When I am afraid, I will put my trust in you" (Ps. 56:3)? Then you came home from school and asked me, "Mommy, what are the words to that song you sing about being afraid?" I told you, and you said, "I have been saying that to myself all day." Oh Katie, you are growing and getting stronger in a lot of ways. Do you ever say that Bible verse now? You have many talents, such as softball, basketball, writing, and you have many friends and a clever sense of humor. You are a very smart girl and very perceptive and are cute and pretty. You know Jesus. Still, you are angry and very sad at times. You are angry at life, divorce, and maybe me. More specifically, you are incredibly sad that your mom and dad aren't married anymore, and you wish that Daddy would be more active in your life and attend your sporting, church, and school events.

I want you to know that you are a blessing to me even when I sometimes yell at you or say dumb things. I always notice your talents and positive traits and am immensely proud of you! (You are still my little girl even if you are taller than me!) Talk to me, Katie, if you want, or talk to your favorite teacher, but always talk to God, for He knows you best. Praying to Him will give you answers, more than you can imagine.

August 2006:

Steve and I got married on August 5, 2006. It was a beautiful and warm summer day as we celebrated our marriage ceremony with a small gathering of family and friends. The pastor from the church where we attended officiated our ceremony. Michael was sixteen, Katie, fifteen, and Nick, Steve's son, was seventeen.

Remarrying and blending two families together, though a positive change, had many adjustments and at times was challenging and stressful. Combining different lifestyles, different temperaments, and different parenting techniques brought unexpected challenges. In spite of the challenges, I'm thankful that we all have blended well in our own distinct ways.

Shortly after Steve and I were married, I began writing in a journal as a gift for him. The journal included various writings. This journal covered a period of six years, and although I didn't write in it often, here is an excerpt from a special and appreciated entry.

May 16, 2011

"The thief comes only to steal, kill, and destroy; I have come that they may have life and have it to the full" (John 10:10).

Steve,

I thank God for our marriage, and I appreciate your sensitive and natural way of expressing your thoughts and feelings. Most importantly, we are growing together and learning more about the Word of God. Today more than ever, Christian marriages are in a battlefield where the enemy is looking for every opportunity to divide them, and we are no exception! In fact, the closer we walk with God individually and as a couple, the more the enemy will try to separate us and destroy our marriage. I so dislike it when we have an argument that causes tension and distance. I am praying for God to search my heart and reveal to me my downfalls in our marriage. It doesn't take me long to figure them out! I trust that God will continue to strengthen us as we seek His will and love one another so that we may glorify Him.

August 5, 2016:

"Perseverance is more than just endurance. It is endurance combined with absolute assurance and certainty that whatever we are looking for is going to happen." Oswald Chambers

Happy Anniversary Steve!

Perseverance is a crucial trait in our marriage. We have worked tirelessly in becoming a stronger team in our efforts to keep God in the center of our relationship. In the ten years of our marriage, we continue to learn the importance of thinking more of one another than ourselves, and practicing the difficult art of patience. We are individuals with shortcomings, but are uniquely made in God's image and know our identity rests solely in Him. Because of our efforts, we can experience a deeper joy in being together. Thank you for your love and commitment that you have put into our marriage. I have complete assurance that whatever we look for in the next phase of our lives, will happen.

This writing was a gift to Steve for our ten-year wedding anniversary. It stems from a lot of work and commitment that we have put into our marriage. Like I wrote: "We have worked tirelessly in becoming a stronger team." This isn't easy for us, and I'll readily admit to that. We each have our strengths and weaknesses in our individual temperaments, and because of that, we sometimes clash and struggle. Then we must work harder. I'm thankful we are willing to work harder. I'm glad both of us have a sense of humor and love to laugh about life and everything that it gives to us—the good times as well as the trying times.

Thoughts and Feelings on High School Graduation

November 2008:
Changes: "Empty Nest"

Everyone experiences changes: young people, middle-aged, and elderly people. Changes can be easy or difficult. They inevitably happen and I'm about to write about the changes I am currently encountering.

People would often talk about "the empty nest syndrome." Of course, having children who were too young at the time, I rarely paid close attention to that saying. I figured I was working enough on their present ages that I could easily wait for them to leave the nest. Well, I am beginning to feel the "empty nest syndrome".

Michael graduated from high school in June and now is a freshman in college at Western Michigan University. He is sensitive and smart, a deep thinker, and deliberate in his thoughts. God has blessed Michael, and I believe He has done great things in his life. It is a very good thing to see. Katie is a senior in high school and has looked into a few different colleges. Huntington University in Indiana seems to be her first choice. She is very independent, bright and strong willed. She has a unique sense of humor that is dry and comical. I saw these traits when she was three years old!

June 2008

Dear Michael,

What wonderful progress and accomplishments you have made! Graduating from high school is certainly an achievement, but you have also experienced some trials that were exceedingly difficult and painful at times. Still, you never gave up. You have excellent friends, and you became a good and strong runner. Most importantly you placed your heart and mind in Jesus Christ. As a result of your determination, God has given you a strong faith and rich knowledge of Him. I know He will continue to do that, for there are no limits to learning about God. For all of these things, I am proud of you and am grateful for you.

On a personal note, you are a fine son, Michael. When you were very young, I saw God beginning to instill in you a desire to learn about the Bible and unfold the rich mysteries found in His Word. Remember when you were in second grade, and I was trying to explain to you that God is in control even when bad and sad things happen? I didn't finish my sentence, and then you quoted Romans 8:28: "And we know that in all things God works for the good of those who love Him, who have been called according to his purpose." Your insight and perception are gifts from God. Use them wisely. Besides always having an inquisitive mind that never can learn enough, you are compassionate, patient, and seem to have a heart for serving others. I'm excited to see the Lord develop and use those traits. College will be a new life, which will bring many changes that may initially seem undesirable. Like other situations you've encountered, you will learn and trust God for yet another step in your life.

Mother's Prayer for a Graduate

God, put them in Your hands, oh those precious children that you've entrusted me with for only a short time. They were mine to raise and for You to see and love and make them who they are supposed to be. But now, I pray for them, please let me cast them into Your hands. May I trust in You.

"Start children off on the way they should go, and even when they are old, they will not turn from it" (Prov. 22:6).

I'll Let You Go, so Don't Fret

July 21, 2009:

When I ask you almost every night where you are going or who you are with, I am not being a domineering mother or treating you as a child, I simply care about you and your safety. You can say I'm protective of you, and I am! But knowing you are safe with the good friends you have chosen gives me peace of mind. So, remember, I'll let you go, so don't fret. When I call you on your cell phone and ask, "Where are you?" you sometimes say, "Why do you care?" It's because I love you and have peace when I know where you are. Remember this, I'm letting you go, so don't fret. When I ask if you work today, don't look at me funny or hesitate to answer. I am not strange; I simply care about you and know this, I'll let you go, so don't fret. When I just want to know where you are, who you are with, or how you are doing, it's because you are my child, my God-given one, since birth. I cannot change that, nor do I wish to. It is always my heart's need to know that you are safe with your friends when you're at work, or wherever you are. I have great peace and joy, knowing you have learned to make right choices in your life for which I am grateful. So, be patient if you can, and give me time to let you go. I love you always and simply want only the best for you. I will let you go, so don't fret.

Do parents ever really let their children go? What does that really mean? Sure, you let them go so they can make decisions on their own as they become more independent. But you don't just release them to the world and never be concerned or worried about them. You pray for them until they are old and gray; you love them as if they still live at home. And you may even cook a meal for them when they are fifty-two! Once you bring a child into the world, they are so often on your mind and always on your heart. There exists a unique kind of parental love that can't be appreciated or comprehended until you become a parent. At times parenting is stressful, but the joys and rewards are always there.

Brokenness

September 2009:

Sometimes you just have to humble yourself and be honest when you want to make something right with someone you love. It's like medicine for the relationship and strength for the soul. Making something right is like putting a broken piece from a beautiful vase back where it belongs, thus making it lovely again.

Thank you, Lord, for Katie. Thank you for our short talk and her willingness to listen, which may help her to feel better. I thank You for your son, Jesus Christ whose body was broken for us on the cross. Because he did this, we can have salvation and some day spend our lives in heaven with Him.

My prayer is that if Katie and Michael ever feel like their heart is broken or close to being so, that they would cry out to the Lord for complete healing. This writing stems from a conversation Katie and I had during some very challenging adjustments after Steve and I got married.

CHAPTER 30

Running the Race to Be Closer to God

February 8, 2011:

I ran on the treadmill, a rare exercise for me, but since it's snowy and icy, I can't run outside. I would much rather be in the pool, swimming laps! Running has never been my aerobic friend, but I've never given myself a chance to like it. This isn't specifically about running, rather it's about climbing a mountain, so to speak, to win the prize of spending eternity with Jesus.

"Do you not know that in a race all the runners run, but only one gets the prize"? Run in such a way to get the prize: (1 Cor. 9:24).

I'm Not a Runner

In August 2019, Katie and I participated in the "Shermanator" at Sherman Lake in Augusta, Michigan. My event comprised of a five-hundred-yard swim, a twelve-mile bike ride, and a 5-K run. Katie did a Duathlon which consisted of a two-mile run, a ten-mile bike ride, and a three-mile run. In early March, I was searching to find a swimming competition and came across this event. I researched it and originally thought Katie, Michael, and I could do it together.

So, I called Katie and told her. "I could do the swimming, you could do the biking, and Michael could do the running."

Her response was, "Why don't you just do all three? You would have to start training now, but you could do it."

I said to Katie, "I'm not a runner."

She replied, "You don't have to be a runner, I'm not a runner." (A couple of years later she ran a marathon!) Okay, then, I thought to myself. Her confidence in me and her natural determination was contagious.

So, training began. Running was what I really needed to focus on because though I was in fairly decent shape, I had never run on a regular basis. Initially, during the training, it was challenging. Until the weather got warm, I used the treadmill but found it to be boring. I began jogging outdoors, which motivated me because I was surrounded by trees, flowers, and the blue sky. Still, I walked more than I ran. I was impatient with my progress, but by late spring and into the summer, I got stronger and improved my form.

In July, after I ran at various tracks, I became really discouraged, thinking, I can't do the running part of this event! I was frustrated because I couldn't run a 5K without stopping. I was close to registering for the Aqua Bike which is a biking and swimming race.

I talked to Michael since he ran cross country in high school and asked him about running on the track versus a park or the neighborhood. I thought running on the track was more difficult. His response was the track's not harder, but it's boring. His one statement sealed it for me, and I finished training at my favorite park. I ran almost every day and loved how I felt afterward and throughout the entire day.

My entire body, especially my brain, greatly benefited from running, and I still like it today. I'm so glad that Katie and I did the Shermanator together. After we finished our races, she said to me, "I told you could do it! You didn't believe me, did you?"

February 2012:
"I wait for the LORD, my whole being waits, and in his word I put my hope" (Ps. 130:5).

I'm frustrated, angry, and disappointed all at the same time. There is so much that I fail to understand, yet much I clearly see. I do know this: this prayer is only for me. I don't want to criticize or try to change anyone. I am asking God to awaken me and discipline me to seriously listen so I may become more like Jesus. God, I want to be still and be able to hear and do Your will. There are many things I desire to do and many changes I want to make but how can those things be accomplished if I don't allow You to begin with me? I will wait for You God, and I will ask for You to give me more love for You and others. I wrote this entry while going through a period of frustration with my work and life in general. I don't have a specific situation. I simply had a desire to be closer to God and do His will in every area of my life.

Draw Near to Your Creator

July 2012:

"Come near to God and he will come near to you" (James 4:8).

One of the most beautiful and powerful gifts that God gives to His children is that the closer we draw to Him, the deeper the relationship becomes. This kind of relationship with the Lord doesn't happen easily or quickly. It doesn't develop by following a three-step manual. By reading His Word and following it and seeking His will for our lives, we thereby draw close to Him. As I spend time with Him by praying, talking to Him, and reading the Bible, I always draw closer to God and then want to share the peace and joy to others that only comes from Him.

CHAPTER 31

Losing Mom

March 6, 2012:

We lost Mom on December 10, 2011. She did not have to suffer, and even though she was diagnosed with cancer several years before her death, she didn't die from cancer. Her health declined when she fell and broke her hip while walking out of church on a Sunday morning. Upon leaving the hospital she went to a nursing home for rehabilitation on her hip.

During Labor Day weekend, and several times before she died, I visited her. She was very happy to see me but was mentally foggy, weak, and anxious at times. She had changed a lot since the last time I visited her. Her memory was poor as she asked the same questions repeatedly and had no recollection of major events or people in my life. She didn't even remember the struggles I had with bipolar disorder. She said to me when I referred to it, "You had depression, Robin?" I was baffled because those years were so crucial and unforgettable for her and our family.

I knew she didn't have Alzheimer's disease, for her issue with memory loss came on so suddenly, and she did not exhibit signs of that particular type of dementia. Still, it was really tough seeing her like this because she became frustrated and was aware of her mental decline. I felt so inadequate. Here I worked with elderly folks on a regular basis, many who had some form of dementia, but I was at a loss of how to respond to her mental and emotional condition.

My last visit with her was during Thanksgiving weekend a couple of weeks before she died. I told Dad that I wanted to spend some time alone with her. He accepted that, and was relieved for it gave him a very much-needed break from caring for and worrying about her. Mom and I talked a little bit, and though she was confused, she seemed peaceful. I combed her hair and put a little makeup on her and she looked pretty for being very ill.

While I was there, I got the mail and noticed there was a letter in the mailbox from Jayne, her husband and daughter, who are very good friends of my family. It was addressed to Mom and Dad. Jayne and her family didn't tell me they were going to send this letter. I opened the letter and read it aloud to my mom.

Dear Jim and Alice,

We had a wonderful time with you all. The pizza was great too! On the way home, I was thinking of how long it had been since we had been together. You all have been in my life since I was born. Wow! Life goes so quickly. Also, on the way home, I was thinking that we may never see each other again on this side of life. We pray that we all meet again in heaven. I love John 3:16: "For God so loved the world that he gave his one and only Son that whoever believes in Him shall not perish but have eternal life." I am so thankful for a sovereign God. I am so

happy to have seen your wedding pictures with my mother and my grandfather in them. It was emotional as I thought about how far back our families go. You are family to me! We pray that you have trusted Jesus Christ as your Savior. We love you all and will keep you in our prayers.
Love, Darren, Jayne, and Kendal

As I read that letter to mom, she looked at me and seemed to have a peace about her. I'm not sure if she was able to understand as I read to her, but God used Jayne and I through a letter to speak to my mom that afternoon. My mom and I had talked a lot about God in the past, and she knew I had trusted Jesus Christ as my Savior when I was twenty years old. I'm so grateful for that letter and Jayne's love for my mother and our family. I know in my heart and mind that its timing wasn't a coincidence, and God knew years later, on that day, I would have an opportunity to read it to her.

"This is good and pleases God our Savior, who wants all people to be saved and to come to a knowledge of the truth" (1 Tim. 2:3–4).

Less than two weeks later, Janice called me to tell me that Mom had taken a major turn for the worse during the evening of December 8. I drove to Lancaster the next day, arrived in the evening, but she had slipped away into a deep sleep. She died the next morning at 5:57.

CHAPTER 32

An Unusual Journal

$\mathcal{B}$eginning in late October 2017 and ending in mid-May 2018, I journaled in a unique way. Inside the cover of this journal, I wrote "Abundance of Thanksgivings to my Lord and Savior Jesus Christ." On the first page I wrote: I am thankful for everything! My plan was to simply write things I was thankful for and nothing else. I got this idea several years ago from my good friend, Harvey, who told me about a book called *One Thousand Gifts* by Ann Voskamp.

"Give thanks in all circumstances; for this is God's will for you in Christ Jesus" (1 Thess. 5:18).

October: 2017:
The Lord has heard my prayer after three months of a trial, and an incredibly unexpected, difficult, and stressful work situation. I waited and prayed and tried to be patient in doing God's will during those months. So, I am giving thanks to God for His faithfulness.

"Consider it pure joy, my brothers and sisters, whenever you face trials of many kinds, because you know that the testing of your faith produces perseverance. Let perseverance finish its work so that you may be mature and complete, not lacking anything" (James 1:2–4).

I'm especially grateful for my dear friend Sandy who recently completed a Bible study on "Putting on the Armor of God." One morning, I shared with her my work situation. She lovingly helped me put this very disturbing situation into prospective by applying scripture, praying with me, and teaching me the necessity of always putting on the full armor of God. There is an adversary always trying to work against the one who trusts in Jesus Christ. I have learned when you put on the full armor of God, Jesus always wins the battle! Ephesians 6:10–12 teaches us: "Finally, be strong in the Lord and in his mighty power. Put on the full armor of God, so that you can take your stand against the devil's schemes. For our struggle is not against flesh and blood, but against the rulers, against the authorities, against the powers of this dark world and against the spiritual forces of evil in the heavenly realms."

I give thanks for God's faithfulness over the last forty years for never leaving me after the initial onset of bipolar disorder.

I am thankful to be able to serve others through the Cancer Hope Prayer List. When I was having a bad day, God renewed my strength when I saw people hurting and suffering from various kinds of cancers. I was involved in a community ministry called Cancer Hope Connections, founded by Margaret, a good friend and cancer survivor. Margaret has a passionate love and empathy to those who have cancer. I was privileged and honor to serve on a very much-needed ministry with a very caring and dedicated team of people.

November 5:

I'm very thankful for my co-workers Angie and Jennifer whom I love. We worked so well together, always striving to love our memory care residents. God brought me to Amber Gardens, and I sometimes miss working with them on a regularly basis, but God's hand was in my transfer to the rehabilitation area. Amber Gardens was a specialized memory care area at Heritage Community of Kalamazoo.

November 8:

I am thankful for my new position at work. The Lord has doubly blessed me. I assist twelve residents with their exercise plan where I work in the physical therapy department. God has already given me peace, and again I clearly see His hand in this change.

I am thankful for my brain that God has fearfully and wonderfully made.

"For you created my inmost being, you knit me together in my mother's womb. I praise you because I am fearfully and wonderfully made; your works are wonderful, I know that full well." (Ps. 139:13–14).

March 2018:

I'm glad to have had tea and lunch with friends in my home. We shared conversation. I also appreciated having tea with some of my co-workers. My hope is for them to see Jesus Christ in my life.

I shared a delicious cinnamon spice tea with a few of my coworkers. The aroma spread throughout the hallways! It was a special and fun moment because several people from other departments smelled the tea, liked it, and ended up buying some. Tara, one of the nurses that I worked with had some of the tea. Back in December, I gave her a Christmas card telling her about my appreciation for her as a person, her work ethic, her love for her children, and her diligent parenting. I told her that I pray for her and her family, which she really appreciated. I also worked with Gloria and Tammy, certified nurse assistants, and we worked very hard and well together.

I'm excited and thankful to share my goal to publish my writings with Katie and Michael, and they are encouraging me to do this. Blessing one: Katie thinks I should do it, and blessing two: she volunteered to be my editor. This brings great joy to me.

Mother's Day

May 2018:

Katie called me this morning to wish me a Happy Mother's Day. I was so delighted and pleased. We had a nice conversation for which I am thankful. The day simply got better as I met Michael and his friend Delaney, and her mother Sharon, for dinner. We had a very nice time.

It's nice that I have been able to live in the moment, something I haven't been able to do lately. Because of this, I am able to appreciate each day as it unfolds.

"The Lord has done it this very day; let us rejoice today and be glad" (Ps. 118:24).

The closer I get to the Lord the more thankful I am for everything.

"Praise the Lord, my soul, all my inmost being, praise his holy name" (Ps. 103:1).

I am medication free from bipolar disorder! I began taking lithium in October 1977. I took it until October 17, 2017. I was on the medication for thirty two of these forty years.

I'm so glad to have completed the gift for my dad, which is a framed collage of pictures of the four seasons with a quote that matches the pictures. This is something I wanted to do in my early twenties. I framed it with the help of my very artistic friends, Val and Sandy.

I'm also thankful for Sylvia, my publishing consultant at Xulon Press. I shared with her that I enjoyed photography, and she encouraged me to give the collage to my dad. I actually wrote this quote in 1983: "It is because of God that we are able to appreciate every season He's created and every season of our lives." I wrote this in appreciation and thanks to God for being free from deep depression. If I wrote that quote today, I would revise it by saying, "It is because of God who made the heavens and earth, that I am able to appreciate every season He's created and every season of my life."

I'm grateful for Madeline, my special friend who is a pianist/accompanist. She and I have been doing musical events at a couple of retirement communities. We thoroughly enjoy the residents. We do a variety of songs from Disney, Gershwin, hymns, and Christmas programs.

I'm grateful to be vacationing at our home in Florida. I'm so glad for this time to relax, enjoy our neighbors, and spend time with Steve. This morning at 7:00, I read an inspiring devotional from *Streams in the Desert 2,* one of my favorite books from Mrs. Charles E. Cowman. In an excerpt of a writing, she wrote: "Christ is the secret, the source, the substance, the center, and the circumference of all true and lasting gladness." I'm grateful in knowing that Jesus is the only true source of peace and joy. Today, it is still a marvelous wonder that He has chosen me.

"For we know, brothers and sisters loved by God, that he has chosen you" (1 Thess. 1:4).

I have peace and contentment in who I am as a woman of faith in God, a mother to my adult children, a wife to Steve, and a servant to the Source who gives all, Jesus Christ.

She is clothed with strength and dignity; she can laugh at the days to come (Prov. 31:25).

CHAPTER 33

Sorrowful and Heartbreaking Losses

January 5, 2019:

We lost Dad to esophageal cancer. He was diagnosed in October 2018, so he had only a few months to battle the disease. In hindsight, my family believes he became ill in August. I was working that day and got a call from Janice at 12:30, saying that his health had taken an unexpected rapid decline. Earlier that morning about 9:00, he began doing poorly during his occupational therapy session. The therapist contacted my sister to tell her that he was not doing well. I left work, went home, and packed a suitcase, and drove to Lancaster, which is a six-hour drive. Jimmy called about 4:30 to say that Dad was doing very poorly and might not survive before I got there. About 6:00, while driving, I got a call from Jimmy saying that Dad had died. Seriously, and quietly I said, "Okay." At that point, I just wanted to safely get to Lancaster and be with the family. I was okay not being there when he died because I didn't want to see him suffer. A few months later, I told my pastor that, and he said, "That was the sovereignty of God." I greatly valued his comment. I learned later that he did not suffer during those last few hours of his life.

In late December, shortly before he died, my dear friend, Charleen, visited Dad while he was at the hospital. He was having some health issues then but was able to return to Crestview rehabilitation and Skilled Nursing Care Center where he was receiving excellent and loving care. Dad always really liked Charleen and appreciated my friendship with her. She has a heart that never stops giving, loving, and caring for others. She genuinely shows her love to her family and friends, and is always eager and ready to share the love of the Lord and the way of salvation with others. She demonstrated that love to my father that day as she spent a couple of hours with him by his bedside. He didn't have a roommate, so she had a special private time with him. She even went to the store to buy him Lifesavers and mints because his mouth was dry. As she held his hand, she prayed with him a beautiful and powerful prayer. He listened and allowed her to do that. The Lord used her that day to care for my dad and pray for him.

Steve, Michael, and Katie arrived in Lancaster on Tuesday, January 8, and we had a nice visitation where many of my friends and my sister and brother's friends attended. The next day we had the funeral, but it really was more like a Celebration of Life service. The pastor gave a meaningful sermon that was positive and uplifting, and scripturally based. He didn't know my father or any of our family personally. When he visited us, he was caring and conscientious about getting to know Dad from the stories and life history that my sister and brother and I gave to him. I was very thankful for him and still am today.

"He will wipe every tear from their eyes. There will be no more death or mourning or crying or pain, for the old order of things has passed away" (Rev. 21:4).

A Shocking and Devastating Loss

Charleen and her husband, Jef, came to the visitation, and Charleen attended Dad's funeral. She sat in the back, so I didn't know she was there until the service was over. She came up to me, and gave me a hug. She went to the cemetery and the luncheon we had for our family and friends. On Thursday January 24, at 6:30 in the morning, Charleen sent me a text message asking if we could talk on the phone. So, I called her, and she told me that she had lost her twenty-one-year-old son, Jaakko on January 23. She was talking very fast, and I believe in shock, understandably so. Jaakko had a history of epilepsy, but at the time, the cause of his death was officially unknown. Charleen and Jef believed his death was seizure related.

A couple of months later, it was confirmed that Jaakko lost his life from SUDEP, sudden unexpected death in epilepsy, which is a fatal complication from epilepsy. He did not suffer and had taken his medication the night that he died which gave Charleen and Jef some comfort. As she did every night, Charleen called him to remind him to take his medication but didn't get an answer. She became concerned, and it was very early on the morning of January 24 that the police came to her home and gave her and Jef the devastating and tragic news. The last words Charleen said to me the morning she told me he had died were, "I just want his life to be a testimony to the Lord." Her wish and hope came true. During his short life, Jaakko loved the Lord, and made a positive difference with people of all ages as he served God faithfully. Though humanly unbearable at times for her and Jef and their other children, family, and many friends, they cling to the hope and promise that they will be with him some day in heaven.

Losing a Lifelong Family Friend and a Special Aunt

March 2020:

We lost Barb, a very close friend of the family, in March of 2020 due to complications from pneumonia. We loved her dearly, and she is missed by so many friends, and family, especially her children and grandchildren. But we all know that because she trusted and loved Jesus as her Savior, she is with Him in heaven.

"We are confident, I say, and would prefer to be away from the body and at home with the Lord" (2 Cor. 5:8).

In late August, my aunt Judy contracted Covid-19, and she died on September 14. This was so unexpected and very sad for me and our family. In early July, she visited Janice, her husband Mark, and their family. As always, Judy enjoyed and appreciated spending time with them. Our family loved her very much. I'm thankful to have video-chatted with her during her visit with the family. Her son Bret, my cousin, tried to keep her home to get her well, but unfortunately, she needed hospital care. Shortly after being admitted, I talked to her on the phone, and though she was tired, she seemed strong and spoke about getting discharged in a few days. With the exception of several text messages and a couple of pictures I sent to encourage her, I didn't talk to her again. She was discharged from the hospital within a couple of weeks and went home under hospice care. She died in the late afternoon, surrounded by Bret, her sister, and other family members.

Refreshing Gifts from God

Sweet Cece

July 2017:

On April 2, our family welcomed Cecelia Lane Shonk, "Cece," into the world. First time parents Kelli and Aaron were extremely happy along with grandparents, Janice and Mark. My Dad was a very proud great-grandpa. In July, I visited the family. Cece was three months old, and it was a special and memorable weekend that I spent with her and her mother. Before she was born, I made a gift for Cece and gave it to Kelli and Aaron. On a sheet of lavender cardstock paper, I typed several verses from Psalm 139 and placed it in a white frame. It was during that weekend the Lord gave me the title of my book. I was reminded of how I am fearfully and wonderfully made, and so is sweet CeCe.

Sweet Cece,
You have searched me; Lord and you know me. You know when I sit and when I rise, you perceive my thoughts from afar. You discern my going out and my lying down; you are familiar with all my ways. Before a word is on my tongue you, Lord, know it completely. You hem me in behind and before, and you lay your hand upon me. Such knowledge is too wonderful for me, too lofty for me to attain.

Where can I go from your spirit? Where can I flee from your presence? If I go up to the heavens you are there; if I make my bed in the depths, you are there. If I rise on the wings of the dawn, if I settle on the far side of the sea, even there your hand will guide me, your right hand will hold me fast. If I say, "Surely the darkness will hide me and the light becomes night around me," even the darkness will not be dark to you, the night will shine like the day, for darkness is as light to you.

For you created my inmost being, you knew me in my mother's womb. I praise you for I am fearfully and wonderfully made; your works are wonderful, I know that full well. My frame was not hidden from you when I was woven together in the depths of the earth. Your eyes saw my unformed body; all the days ordained for me were written in your book before one of them came to be. How precious to me are your thoughts, God! How vast is the sum of them! Were I to count them, they would outnumber the grains of sand-when I am awake, I am still with you. (Ps. 139:1–18)

November 20, 2019:

Elliot Mae Shonk was born and made her big sister, Cece, along with her parents and the rest of our family thankful to God. She is a healthy and happy baby. I met Elliot for the first time shortly after Christmas. Katie and I visited, and Katie was able to be with her two second cousins. I gave the same gift to Elliot that I had given to Cece. The white frame contained several verses from Psalm 139 with a special emphasis on verses

13–14. The cardstock paper was mint green to match the color of her bedroom.

> For you created my inmost being,
> You knit me together in my mother's womb.
> I praise you because I am fearfully and wonderfully made.
> Your works are wonderful, I know that full well.
> (Ps. 139:13–14)

May 2020:

Nick, my stepson and his wife Ali, had their first baby, Riley Jean Haverkamp, on May 3. Due to Covid-19, we haven't had much contact but are enjoying pictures, videos, and brief visits with her. She is a very cheerful, sweet, and adorable blessing to her thankful and delighted parents. Steve and I, proud grandparents, look forward to spending more time with her.

A Trustworthy, Loved and Appreciated Friendship

November:

"Two are better than one, because they have a good return for their labor. If either one of them falls down, one can help the other up." (Eccles 4:9) ; "So, do not fear for I am with you; do not be dismayed, for I am your God." "I will strengthen you and help you; I will uphold you with my righteous right hand" (Isa. 41:10).

In 2012, Steve met a man named Leon. One day, Leon was walking in our neighborhood, looking for work. He carried a flyer that described his job description, which was a repair person/landscaper. He was extremely handy and skilled at his work, and very dedicated. Because of health issues, he was not able to work full time. Steve and he began talking, and they completed several projects in our home. Through the years, they became close friends, and their work relationship developed into a special, valued friendship. They were thankful to God for allowing their paths to cross. I loved and appreciated Leon and enjoyed being with him and always respected the close friendship he and Steve had.

Leon grew up in a foster home with caring and loving parents. Though he faced many physical and mental challenges, he was always thankful and valued each moment of life that God gave to him, especially as his health issues worsened. He was friendly, kind, caring, and always eager to help and serve others, particularly those who needed his skilled services.

In October, while Steve and I were on a short vacation, Leon called Steve from the hospital, saying he had contracted Covid-19. Because of his underlying serious health issues, both Steve and I were concerned but hopeful that he may recover. Like a lot of people who get this virus, he initially sounded fairly strong. But, after several calls that Steve and I had with him, he no longer was able to compete with the fierce virus. On November 21, we lost a trustworthy and very beloved friend. In spite of his health issues, Leon often said, "I'm blessed!" Today, we appreciate and are thankful for his steadfast faith in the Lord.

CHAPTER 34

A Surprising and Difficult Season

"I waited patiently for the LORD; he turned to me and heard my cry. " (Ps. 40:1).

February–May 2021:

I experienced an unexpected stretch of depression the latter part of February. Initially, my mood was unusually hyper; I was physically restless, and extraordinarily anxious. Covid-19 restrictions affected the ability to see my family. At work I had to witness my special and extraordinarily strong residents being separated from their loved ones, accelerating my troubles. Life began to spin out of control. Wearing a mask at work became very tiring, and I was getting headaches which I rarely if ever get.

I'm grateful for our team of leaders and the staff from every department at Heritage Community of Kalamazoo. They worked tirelessly to keep a low percentage of residents and staff from contracting the virus. It was still difficult and upsetting for me to see the residents and their loved ones endure the hardships that accompanied the virus.

Working on my manuscript and having an obsessive need to finish it before my vacation in March escalated my mood. I devoted a lot of time to writing the last couple of years but especially during the fall of 2020. During this time I wrote almost every day before I went to work, but I was always hurrying and going too fast in almost everything I was doing.

On March 5, Steve and I were leaving for vacation, and my sister-in-law was going to visit us, so I didn't want to work on the manuscript during that time. I called a few of my close friends, asking them to pray that I would have it completed by March 4. I didn't really think I was, but looking back, I now know I was experiencing symptoms of moderate depression which included difficulty in thinking, concentrating and making decisions. I lost interest in things I enjoyed doing and found it tiring and difficult to socialize with my family and friends.

One evening while at work, I was feeling stressed and down, so I took my break in the dining room. I listened to an excerpt of a sermon from Philippians 4:4–7 from my pastor and teacher/expositor David Thompson.

Rejoice in the Lord always. I will say it again: Rejoice! Let your gentleness be evident to all. The Lord is near. Do not be anxious about anything, but in every situation, by prayer and petition, with thanksgiving, present your requests to God. And the peace of God, which transcends all understanding, will guard your hearts and your minds in Christ Jesus.

His teaching of these verses was effective and encouraging. He said many things, but one statement that clearly stood out to me was: "When you're depressed, talk to God!" A peace came over me because I do that and have done it since I was twenty years old. During that short, twenty-minute break, I found much encouragement and strength, and I learned to trust in the Lord and his timing in completing the manuscript.

"He has made everything beautiful in its time" (Eccles. 3:11).

CHAPTER 35

Fulfilling the Vision

When and Why, I Decided to Publish My Writings.

"Then I heard the voice of the Lord saying, 'Whom shall I send? And who will go for us?' And I said, 'Here I am. Send me!' (Isa. 6:8).

In 2012, I began seriously questioning what I should do with all of my journals that were sitting on my bookshelf, going nowhere. True, a few years back, I began working on some writings that I had written in various journals through the years. Still, I was anxious and wrestled with the thought of what I should do with all of these journals that I had written in since I was fourteen! There is one thing that I was sure of, and that is since I was in my early twenties, I wanted to help others who suffer with depression. I deeply yearned to make a positive and effective difference and tell others about the amazing grace and love that God had given to me. My desire was to share that they, too, could have a peace, strength, and hope that only God can give through a personal relationship with Jesus Christ.

A few years passed, and then I got my answer. Clearly this is what came to my mind: "If you want to publish your writings, you have to fully embrace the brain that I gave to you." It was a clear direction from God that gave me peace, made sense, and answered the question of what I should do with my journals.

I've never been ashamed of having bipolar disorder, but that topic just doesn't come up in everyday conversation, and I didn't share it with just anyone. So, in some regards, I was unsure and uncomfortable in telling people about it. Realistically speaking, there is a stigma attached to mental illness. I have heard many people through the years who simply do not have an accurate understanding of this particular mental illness. I hear people in social gatherings or in my work setting who nonchalantly comment about someone having bipolar disorder when the person is happy one minute and sad or angry the next. I know a couple of those people they are referring to, and they clearly do not exhibit symptoms of this illness. In addition, there are those who unfortunately are misdiagnosed with this mood disorder by a doctor or a counselor.

Beginning in 1983, I trusted Jesus Christ as my Savior, and He opened my heart and mind to write about people, places, family, friends and events. I especially wanted to glorify God through my writings since He's the one who gave me new physical and spiritual life.

In June 2017, I decided it was time to publish. I had a clear direction from God to begin the process, adventure, and journey to complete what I had started in my early twenties. I was finally going to do what I wanted to do. Through my forty years of journaling I could write about the amazing acts and miracles which God performed in my life. I also could hopefully help others with bipolar disorder or other types of depression.

Finding a Publisher

"Being confident in this, that he who began a good work in you will carry it on to completion until the day of Christ Jesus" (Phil. 1:6).

June 7, 2017:

A few years back, I bought two blank-page books at the Christian bookstore. I had no intentions of journaling in them but thought I would give them as gifts to my friends. I ended up using one of those books, and on the first page I wrote: Goal: To publish a book, a devotional, or whatever it may be called to glorify God. It was finally time for me to publish my writing, so I researched publishing companies and found one I thought I wanted to work with. I spoke with a publishing consultant and learned a little about the process. A few days later, I realized that publishing company wasn't the right one and that I needed to do more research. As I became anxious, impatient, and concerned, I thought about a good friend, Susie, who published her book. The title was *We Are the Much More*. I went to my library and pulled her book off the shelf and looked to see who her publisher was. I read "Xulon Press."

I did a little research and the next day at work during my lunch break I called Xulon Press" and talked with a publishing consultant named Sylvia. In less than a half hour, I told her how I wanted to turn my journal entries into a book. I talked fast and was in a hurry, but Sylvia was kind, calm, and professional. She had a sweet confidence about the publishing company she worked for. We made an appointment to discuss my plan to publish in further detail. What initially began as a short conversation blossomed into a very special relationship, one that was professional, individualized, and incredibly helpful.

It didn't take long for me to learn that she cared deeply about my dream to publish my writings and share God's amazing grace and wonders in my life. At times when it was overwhelming to figure out what journal entries to include in the book, Sylvia reminded me of my goal by saying "Write what Glorifies God and helps others."

In 2018, Steve and I met Sylvia while vacationing in Florida. Her office was less than two hours from our home. How convenient and providential! We had a productive meeting in which I talked about my book, my dream I had to publish, and certain things I wanted in the book. Steve asked many important questions as he always does, for which I am thankful. After more meetings with Sylvia, many prayers and planning, we decided to do this. In August 2020 it was officially settled. I was on the road to getting my writings published.

Chapter 36

Unforeseen Lab Work

*I*n 2015, I had routine lab work done. With the exception of eight years, I had taken lithium since I was seventeen. This particular medication, like some others, can cause damage to the kidneys. I got my lab results back, and my renal function numbers were mildly elevated. I had an ultrasound done, and it revealed kidney damage from lithium use. My doctor wasn't concerned and didn't think I needed to see a nephrologist at that time. He still referred me to one to see if I needed to take a different medication that would not cause further damage to the kidneys. Without consulting my physician, I chose to cut back on the medicine and began taking a fairly low dose of it. Because of the reduced dose of the medicine, I eventually got confused on how much I was taking so began having noticeable symptoms of mania: decreased need of sleep and then insomnia, and racing thoughts, all of which were frightening. I recognized what had happened. It took a few days to get back on track, but I did, thank God. I continued to take a low dose of lithium on a consistent basis, and felt strong again.

Saying Goodbye to Lithium

In October 2017, I thought it wise to see a psychiatrist and learn about a medication that would be safer for my kidneys. I was in college the last time I saw a specialist, so it was like a new experience seeing one again. The appointment went very well, and the doctor was extremely helpful and understanding of my mental health history and my questions about taking a different medication. I stopped taking lithium, and she prescribed lamictal, a mood stabilizer that is used to treat bipolar disorder.

When she recommended it, Steve and I looked at each other and smiled because when we researched medications, that was the one we thought might be safe and effective. The doctor informed us that there were very few side effects. The most common one being a skin rash. I began taking it, but within two weeks, I developed a rash, called the doctor, and was told to discontinue it immediately, so I did. I decided to wait to see how I felt before going back to the doctor to try another medication. Three months later, I got the same rash! I couldn't understand it since I wasn't taking lamictal. The rash was in the same place; on my left temple where my bangs swept over my forehead. Then it dawned on me that I developed the rash from the hair color I used! It was a different one that I had not used, and three months later, used it again and got the same allergic reaction. The interesting thing about it is that for three months I wasn't taking any medication and felt strong and well. So, how does anyone explain this?

During my appointment, the doctor told me that there was a hormonal factor relating to my mental health history. At age fourteen, I had the onset of bipolar disorder (hormonal). Both times when I was pregnant per my doctor's order, I didn't take any lithium and felt fine (hormonal). Then when I was in my mid-forties, I began having mild to moderate depression, irritability, and mild memory issues. These issues, caused by perimenopause (hormonal), were interrupting my life. Thankfully, I recognized the symptoms and told my general physician. He prescribed a low dose of a safe and effective medication which I took for about a year giving me minimal side effects.

In October 2022, It will be five years since I have taken lithium. Today I am not taking any medication for bipolar disorder. I still experience symptoms of it if I don't properly take care of my body. In order to be at my best mentally, physically, and emotionally, I need to get adequate rest, which is seven or eight hours of sleep. If I don't slow my brain down at a certain time in the evening, it's very challenging for me to fall asleep. My energy level is more intense, I have racing thoughts, I talk faster and incessantly, which my family and friends would say is normal for me! Life's stressors, positive and negative, magnify these symptoms. I drink a tea that helps me sleep well and also take an herbal supplement which is effective. Eating a healthy diet, drinking minimal caffeine, and exercising regularly are also crucial for me to feel strong and well. I'm not perfect at doing all of these things and at times far from it. When I fail, I quickly get back on track. To me, the human brain is an amazing organ that God created, and I appreciate the importance of taking care of it just like any other organ of the body. Most importantly, I choose God to enable me to manage bipolar disorder.

The Great Physician and Perfect Counselor

God is the perfect Counselor and Great Physician as I try to seek His will every day and read the Bible. The Word of God has every answer I need to live a healthy and productive life.

For unto us a child is born, to us a son is given, and the government will be on his shoulders. And he will be called Wonderful Counselor, Mighty God, Everlasting Father, Prince of Peace. (Isa. 9:6)

None is like you LORD; you are great, and your name is mighty in power. (Jer. 10:6)

When I was twenty years old, He gave me the gift of His grace, love, and forgiveness; the perfect package of salvation. I talk to Him, pray to Him, and sing to Him. I love Him. If I went to a physician today and said I was having symptoms of depression or mania, a medication would be prescribed to treat my symptoms, and I understand that, looking at it from a medical perspective. Personally, I have chosen to not take lithium or any other medication. In the early to mid-eighties when I didn't take the medication, I simply trusted God to help me. It's not like I felt fine; in fact, as I wrote in my journals, there were occasions when I had a difficult time keeping my moods balanced. I trusted God and believed He would always help me. He gave me an unwavering faith that remains in me today.

"Now faith is confidence in what we hope for and assurance about what we do not see." (Heb. 11:1).

I'm not saying that when you trust in Him, you will never have depression, bipolar disorder, or any other mental health condition. That simply isn't realistic, nor is it stated in the Bible that Christians are exempt from it. I have close friends who have a saving faith in Jesus Christ and struggle at times with some kind of depression, and they take medication. I also know they have hope, strength, and joy when they pray to God, allowing Jesus to intercede on their behalf. He fully understands and knows every trial we face in this life. He endured and agonized over the deepest sadness, grief, darkness, and physical pain. Regardless of any form of suffering encountered, no human being will ever encounter the level of mental anguish and physical pain that Jesus Christ did. I can't fathom that level of suffering but know that He did it for me and the entire human race when He was severely tortured and crucified on the cross. I have a deep belief that comes from personal experience that there is no level of depression that God can't manage, put into a healthy perspective, and greatly use to glorify Him.

"No, in all these things we are more than conquerors through him who loved us. For I am convinced that neither death nor life, neither angels nor demons, neither the present, nor the future, nor any powers, neither height, nor depth, nor anything else in all creation, will be able to separate us from the love of God that is in Christ Jesus our Lord"(Rom. 8:37-39).

I am beyond thankful to have a personal relationship with my heavenly Father, and knowing that Jesus Christ is always interceding on my behalf allows me to greatly appreciate and accept the brain that He has given to me. I have complete assurance, knowledge, peace and joy in knowing that I am fearfully and wonderfully made.

CHAPTER 37

Teen Depression and Suicide

A few years ago, while I was at work during a lunch break, a coworker shared with me about her best friend losing her thirteen-year-old daughter to suicide. I simply listened while she poured her heart out to me. On another occasion, one of my coworkers shared with me that her teenage daughter had been taking some over-the-counter pain pills, thinking it would help her anxiety and depression. Fortunately, her parents discovered this and immediately sought help for her.

I later followed up with my coworker and was glad and relieved to hear that her daughter was moving in a healthier direction and doing well. Suicide does not discriminate for there is no age group which is immune. I have a special compassion for teenagers who have committed suicide, and unfortunately, there are countless stories of this tragic and unnecessary cause of death. When I hear or read these stories, my heart bleeds for those teenagers, their parents, and their loved ones. The deep concern and empathy I have comes from my personal experience of wanting to take my life during the summer of 1981.

At eighteen after experiencing deep depression, I remember thinking that people don't want to die; they simply want to be strong and live well. They just want the issue causing deep depression to go away. For me, I remember thinking I can't live in continual darkness where I was mentally and emotionally dysfunctional. Some of the reasons that teens take their lives today are not necessarily the same reasons that I wanted to take mine. My depression was clinical, an imbalance in my brain. I had more internal troubles than external ones. Today, there are so many more external pressures causing teen depression.

Teens in the U.S. continue to experience increased rates of depression and anxiety, resulting in a rise of self-harm and death by suicide. Technology and social media may play a role, according to a recent study. Dr. Angela Mattke, a Mayo Clinic pediatrician not involved in the study, helps explain the connection.

Computers, laptops, smartphones all play an important role in the lives of our teens. Dr. Mattke says teens are "using [technology] to learn in the classroom and out of the classroom. They're using it to collaborate and connect on projects." But it's outside the classroom where too much social media may lead to social problems. Dr. Mattke says kids learn to become passive engagers. "They're watching everyone else's Instagram, but they're not engaging and, so, they're losing out on that social connection. "Electronic screens also can disrupt sleep. And a lack of good sleep can result in a depressed mood, moodiness, and irritability. "If they are spending a lot of time on their cellphones or screens, it can affect the hormones in their brain via the blue light that comes off of these screens."

"Is a Rise in Teen Depression Linked to Technology, Social media?" Deb Balzer, 2019

CHAPTER 38

The Benefits of Journaling

I believe that journaling has become more popular in the last fifteen years than it was when I began journaling in the late seventies. In 2006, I went shopping for a journal and needed to go to several stores before I could find one, and even then, there wasn't much of a selection. Finally, I found one that I liked at a bookstore.

Today, journals are easy to find. I see them at gift shops, bookstores, department stores, office supply stores, and even some grocery stores in the stationery section. I remember I kept a diary for a very short time when I was nine, and then at thirteen, I wrote a couple of sentences in a spiral ring notebook.

One year later, I began consistently journaling while in the hospital. I began writing because of one teacher who brought one rose and one red journal with golden trim around it. I will always remember that moment. I began then and never stopped writing. I wrote mostly before I went to sleep at night but many times during the day. When I rode my bike to the park, I tucked my journal in my backpack. There were few places where I didn't have it with me. There was an incessant need to write my thoughts and feelings about people, places, and events.

Later after I believed in and received Jesus Christ as my Savior, I wrote about miracles, trials, my sins, and amazing and wonderful experiences with people. The never-ending grace, love, and forgiveness is woven throughout the pages of many years of journaling. As I reviewed my journals, I've been able to see how it has incredibly benefited me physically and emotionally. Furthermore, I have a written account and journey of God's wonderous love and redemption in my life. The beauty of seeing His work in leading me through and managing bipolar disorder will always amaze me. I will forever appreciate my new life in His Son Jesus Christ.

A few years ago, I researched the benefits of journaling and discovered several articles on the subject. I was happy to read the benefits from the sources I gathered. I smiled because I am thankful to say that I have reaped the advantages of journaling. I had no idea that when I began over forty years ago, I would experience those benefits.

Five Powerful Health Benefits of Journaling

What are some of the short- and long-term health benefits

1. Reduces Stress. An overabundance of stress can be damaging to your physical, mental, and emotional health. It's proven. Journaling is an incredible stress management tool, a good-for-you habit that lessens impact of physical stressors on your health.

2. Improves Immune Function. Believe it or not, expressive writing can strengthen your immunity and decrease your risk of illness. Those who journal boost improved

immune system functioning (strengthens immune cells), as well as lessened symptoms of asthma and rheumatoid arthritis. Expressive writing has been shown to improve liver and lung function and combat certain diseases; it has even been reported to help the wounded heal faster.

3. Keeps Memory Sharp. Journaling helps keep your brain in tip-top shape. Not only does it boost memory and comprehension, but it also increases working memory capacity, which may reflect improved cognitive processing.

4. Boosts Mood. Want more sunshine in your life? Try journaling. A unique social and behavior outcome of journaling is this: It can improve your mood and give you a greater sense of overall emotional well-being and happiness.

5. Strengthens Emotional Functions. Related to mood is how journaling benefits overall emotional health: As journaling habits are developed, benefits become long-term, meaning that diarists become more in tune with their health by connecting with inner needs and desires. Journaling evokes mindfulness and helps writers remain present while keeping perspective. It presents an opportunity for emotional catharsis and helps the brain regulate emotions.

"Five Powerful Health Benefits of Journaling, "Kasee Bailey, 2018

FIVE REASONS TO JOURNAL DAILY

JOURNALING ENABLES US TO CHRONICLE OUR JOURNEY WITH CHRIST

JOURNALING HELPS US PROCESS OUR THOUGHTS AND EXPERIENCES.

JOURNALING REMINDS US OF GOD'S FAITHFULNESS.

JOURNALING KEEPS US FOCUSED ON GOD'S WORD.

JOURNALING IS A HELPFUL DISCIPLINE THAT KEEPS US

COMING BACK, DAY AFTER DAY, TO THE WORD.

WELL-WATERED WOMEN ARTICLES, GRETCHEN SAFFLES, MARCH 2021

Chapter 39

Significant and Cherished Writings

*T*he following writings were mostly written during the years of 2009–2018 with the exception of a few written in the 1980s. I wrote so many journal entries over the past forty years comprised of stories, reflections, and Christian writings.

A Very Special Boy and His Family

December 24, 1984:

God, please help him with this illness that he's had for so long. Continue to give him, his parents, and his family, strength and courage to fight this battle. May they rely on you during a humanly unbearable time. Let their hearts feel peace in knowing that you have his life in your hands. Eric was a boy I babysat along with his two brothers, Adam and John. I began babysitting this family when I was fifteen and continued into my early twenties. When Eric the was two years old, he was diagnosed with leukemia and courageously fought his illness with the constant love from his family and friends. He bravely lost his battle when he was eight years old. I had several families I babysat for and loved all of the children and their parents, but this family was particularly special to me. Through the years of babysitting for Mandy and Glen's sons, we became close friends and still are today. Whenever I'm in Lancaster, I'm so glad when we can get together. Their faith in the Lord was especially evident during the years of Eric's illness. This faith was admirable and amazing to me.

A Painful Regret

November 19, 1986:

I felt sad tonight toward the end of the church service. I thought back to when I was very upset with my dad and said something cruel and unkind. I felt so miserable that night, and it still bothers me from time to time. I regret saying it, and I'm sure it hurt him. Has he gotten over it or forgiven me? I asked God to forgive me. What can I do to change it? I called him tonight and told him I loved him and apologized, but what I'd like to do is write to him and tell him that I am sorry. Shortly after I apologized to my father, I wrote a poem and gave it to him. He appreciated it, and we became closer. He often saved special cards and notes from me and my siblings, but I didn't know if he had kept this particular poem. Many years later my brother retrieved it for me. It was in an envelope with other cards and notes I had given to him. I was so glad and thankful that he had saved that particular writing because it was a confirmation that it meant a lot to him.

Love and Forgiveness from My Earthly Father and Heavenly Father

The Love of a Father to His Daughter
is the kind of love that a daughter can't quite
understand which is the
Kind that is always there to hold her hand.
It's the kind of love that is still so true
Through the storms of life that cause her heart to feel so blue.
It's the kind of love that rejoices and shares a smile with her,
though at times she could not
Show one for a while.
Even after mistakes have been made,
it's the kind of love that never
Quits trying, though at times I'm sure she felt like crying.
Oh yes, it's the kind of love that hopes
for the best in the daughter he loves
And desires from his heart to do his part in making her happy
Through her entire life.
For without you, Dad, my life and character would be
Incomplete, on which to live a strong foundation that you
have helped me successfully build
With a fatherly love behind every tool that was used.
What is this love that from birth comes
so naturally to a father?
It is the love of a father to his daughter.
So, this is my hope and prayer
That you will recognize today, my love for you is oh,
so strong in many ways.
With love and gratitude, Robin

In 2017, after my niece, Kelli, and her husband, Aaron, had their first baby, Cecelia Lane, I visited my family. It was a joyous occasion as we welcomed this precious baby girl into our world. My dad was very proud to be a great-grandfather for the first time. During that weekend, he and I had a nice and special visit, one which I will always remember and hold close within my heart. I was at his home, and he sat in his glider chair which he really liked. I sat directly across from him on the blue sofa.

We began talking about different things like family with a special emphasis on the birth of Cece, friends, Mom, and just life in general. We talked about Michael and Katie, and that they were doing well. He also asked about Sarah and Ryen. Even though he hadn't seen them in several years, he loved them and cared about them, and hoped their lives were going well. Then our discussion became really serious. He spoke of the difficult times that my kids and I experienced during my post-divorce years. I told him that as Michael and Katie entered their twenties, I would periodically talk to them individually about those years.

I then told him that for several years, I didn't feel like a good mother, even though I knew I had done my best in loving and caring for the kids. I continued by saying I was able to manage with the strong emotional support of the family in addition to the financial support that he and Mom had given to me. Then I got emotional, and my eyes watered. It was at that moment that my dad quickly looked directly at me over his reading glasses as if he were staring into my heart and soul. He said to me in a very serious and caring tone: "Robin, I probably didn't tell you this enough during those years, but you were a good mother." Those words brought much comfort to me. I held back the tears because I didn't want either one of us, especially him, to feel sad.

Over thirty years have passed since I gave that poem to my dad. Today I can't help but think of an analogy of God, my heavenly Father, and His love to me. As my dad looked up at me with a facial expression of love and care, I thought about my heavenly Father who loves and cares about me with a love I cannot fully comprehend.

"See what great love the Father has lavished on us, that we should be called children of God!" (1 John 3:1). "How precious to me are your thoughts, God! How vast are the sum of them! Were I to count them, they would outnumber the grains of sand. When I awake, I am still with you." (Ps. 139:17–18).

A Beloved Friendship from the Lord

July 19, 1987:
"I always thank my God as I remember you in my prayers, because I hear about your love for all his holy people and your faith in the Lord Jesus." (Philem. 1:4–5).

Thank you, God, for creating peace and joy in my evening because earlier I felt afraid and discouraged. I thank you for Charleen and our special friendship. I know it was your plan to give it to us and what's more beautiful than when you bring two of your children together for strength and love? Charleen and I first met when I worked at Gloria Marshalls, a woman's exercise facility. We were in our early twenties. She exercised there, and we quickly became friends and remain close today. In 1985, I had a small journal in which I wrote prayers and praises to God. Charleen wrote a powerful and heartfelt prayer for me in that little book. In 2017, I showed it to her, and this was the first time she read it since she had written this heartfelt prayer.

For Robin, I pray, Lord, that she will keep the faith she has and will continue to renew her faith and strengthen it by reaching out to others, as she is always doing. Give her confidence that will make her develop her talents given by You. She is so rare and unique in that in Your image, she has grown fully alive and fully capable of spreading Your love and peace. Help her to remember that Your power is already in her, and all she has to do is conquer all doubts, fears, and confusions. In Jesus' Holy name, help her to influence others in Your abiding love. In Jesus' name, Amen.

I Want to Go Home

August 2017:

In my work as a certified nurse assistant, I have spent much time with folks who have dementia, particularly those who suffer with Alzheimer's Disease. I have seen people who are pleasantly confused and others who are angry and at times verbally and physically combative.

I believe one thing they all have in common is that the world in which they live is a sad and hopeless one. One phrase I often hear is "I want to go home." Their present home is not the home they are longing for. People who are in the later stages of the disease, sometimes live in a specialized care center. When I hear the plea of wanting to go home, that is real and true to the person suffering from a cruel emotional, mental, and physical disease. This longing has always been difficult for me to hear. Even my training and experience dealing with this situation doesn't diminish the compassion I feel for these people suffering with Alzheimer's Disease. My empathy runs deep.

When I was in the hospital back in 1977, I badly wanted to go home. I remember saying to my doctor as he sat on the edge of my bed. "I want to go home." I was recovering but wasn't well enough to return to my home and be with my family and friends in Lancaster. I didn't understand the full complexity of the story as to why I was in the hospital. So, when I hear my residents say I want to go home, I understand it, and my heart aches for them. It's so sad to me because in the later stages of the disease, most won't ever again see their home and cannot grasp why they can't go home. The dynamics between me and these folks are different, but there is a parallel. I was very confused, had memory lapses, and was out of touch with reality just like many people who suffer with Alzheimer's Disease. The striking difference is that they can't go home, but I could, and I did!

Jesus answered, "Everyone who drinks this water will be thirsty again, but whoever drinks the water I give them will never thirst. Indeed, the water I give them will become in them a spring of water welling up to eternal life" (John 4:13–14).

A Waterfall of Love and Strength

February 2018:

I really like water. I like drinking it, splashing cool water on my face, swimming in pools and lakes, and I particularly like swimming in Lake Michigan. I especially like waterfalls, watching them and swimming under them. When my husband and I were on a vacation, we visited a resort where there was a strong and powerful waterfall going into the pool. Before I got in the pool to enjoy swimming under it, I looked at it and had a peaceful and relaxing moment. From a distance, it looked playful and scenic, but as I approached it and eventually dove into it, this scenic waterfall was actually forceful and surprisingly powerful, exhilarating, and refreshing. What did I realize? The waterfall to me symbolized God's strength and power in my life. It reminded me of some of God's characteristics: Wonder, power, and grace. As much as I enjoy water in its various forms, nothing compares to the living water of eternal life given by Jesus Christ.

Waterfall

Oh God, my God, I seek you
I wanna move when you move
You're more than I could long for

I thirst for you
You're an ocean to my soul to my soul.

Your love is like a waterfall, waterfall
Running wild and free. Chris Tomlin, 2014

What Motivates You?

March 23, 2017

One afternoon, I surprised my daughter, Katie, on her birthday while she was working. It was a beautiful but chilly sunny day. As we were having lunch, we talked about personalities. I described her temperament as independent and strong willed. I told her that she was naturally assertive and believed it served her well, especially as she experienced extraordinarily difficult and painful times during childhood. Intrigued, she told me that those are two traits that described her as she had learned through a personality study.

We discussed my personality, and we agreed that people are born with a temperament, and various things including people influence us and shape us to be who we are. I said that I'm an extravert and love people, but I also like and need solitude. She responded in reference to her temperament study by saying it goes deeper than that. We both agreed that it's really what motivates you to be the person you are.

On my way home from my visit with Katie, I was thankful for our time together. I began thinking that yes, I do love people, and enjoy life but it's really God who motivates me to love others, even when at times it's a challenge! It's his love that abides in me, lives in me, and flows out of me. "Dear friends, since God so loved us, we also ought to love one another" (1 John 4:11).

Hazel, an Exquisite Woman

May 19, 2011:

   A woman of unshakeable faith
   A woman of brilliance and sensitivity
   A woman who deeply appreciates literature, stories, poems, and Bible scriptures
   A woman who wants to keep learning as much as she can until the moment she leaves this life
   A woman who cannot see with human eyes but deeply understands the human soul
   A woman of timeless perseverance, character, and wisdom
   A woman of godly traits with an amazing memory of God's perfect Word and promises

Hazel, a beautiful woman who savors every minute of life until she takes her last breath.

Hazel was a resident I knew at a care facility. She was blind from an illness but in spite of her limitations she had a deep appreciation for life and her relationship with Jesus Christ. I had several one-on-one visits with her. What a kind, caring, and wise woman she was. I believe we were a blessing to one another. She was often resting in her bed, so she couldn't attend the hymn sings or variety shows in which I participated. Even though she wasn't able to attend a music event, Hazel would often say to me with such optimism, "I still want to hear you sing!"

"Brothers and sisters, I do not consider myself yet to have taken hold of it. But one thing I do: Forgetting what is behind and straining toward what is ahead, I press on toward the goal to win the prize for which God has called me heavenward in Christ Jesus" (Phil. 3:13–14).

Pressing forward: Letting Go of Past Pain

There are times when it is difficult letting go of pain because I tend to obsessively dwell on the past. It's been a process to go forward and will always be a work in progress, but I'm so glad I have learned how incredibly futile it is to dwell on negative past events.

"Forget the former things; do not dwell on the past. See I am doing a new thing! Now it springs up; do you not perceive it? I am making a way in the wilderness and streams in the wasteland" (Isa. 43:18–19).

Some Day It Will All Be Over

Summer, 2011:

It's okay; someday it will all be over. How vividly I recall saying those words to myself, as I was raising two young children as a single parent. I knew that God was leading me through an incredibly difficult journey after the devastating effects of an alcoholic marriage. There was much confusion, sadness, anger, and loneliness for me and the children. Often, the grief was painful and almost humanly impossible to bear.

I just reminded myself that someday either the Lord would reach down from the clouds in heaven and I would go with him, or I would experience physical death and be with Him. "After that, we who are still alive and are left will be caught up together with them in the clouds to meet the Lord in the air. And so, we will be with the Lord forever" (1 Thess. 4:17). Either way, my home would be in heaven. Then the emotional pain would disappear, and all of those horrible feelings and memories would finally be gone. God's promises in His Word are absolutely true, and I knew He was the mighty Counselor, and my hope was in Him.

As time passed and my heart began to heal, I became stronger and able to cope with the grief and pain that had been difficult to erase from my memory. The children began to pass through the deep waters of brokenness as well. I saw the fruits academically, athletically and in youth group events at church. I stopped longing for the time when "It would all be over."

A few years back, Michael and I had a discussions about some very difficult things that happened when he was growing up, which were difficult for me to let go. During one of the discussions, his response was, "Mom, that was nine years ago."

Michael has a way of calmly summarizing some of life's situations by saying just a few words. He has helped me put things into perspective for which I am grateful.

Katie is naturally good at moving forward and letting go of the past. She is assertive, brave, and in her caring nature, will tell me not to worry about things that don't matter and have already happened. These personality traits have helped her through extremely painful experiences. I'm so proud of her, and together we have learned how strong and courageous we are. I value Michael and Katie's God-given temperaments.

A Deeper Understanding and Knowledge of the Word of God

In August 2016, Steve and I began attending services at Texas Corners Bible Church. We continue to worship there today. It only took a few visits for us to like the teaching of Pastor David E. Thompson, the friendly people and positive atmosphere in the church. In June 2017, I was hospitalized for a serious illness. I got an infection which I did not know the severity of, and within forty-eight hours what seemed treatable with an antibiotic turned septic.

I am so grateful to have had excellent care and to have fully recovered from a potentially life-threatening illness. During a six-day hospital stay, Pastor David visited me twice. I was appreciative of his pastoral care and his prayer for me. There were people at the church Steve and I didn't even know who prayed for me during the weekly prayer meeting led by Mary, David's wife.

I'm especially grateful for Pastor Thompson's teaching on Paul's verses in the Bible about letting go of the past and pressing forward. A few years ago, I asked him if I could meet with him because I had a few things I wanted to discuss. During those meetings, I told him about some difficult experiences in my life. He cared and listened but wisely suggested that I let go of those things and gave me a couple of Bible verses that specifically taught about letting go and moving forward.

Steve and I are so pleased and thankful that we worship at Texas Corners Bible Church. We deeply appreciate the extraordinary gift that God has given to Pastor Thompson as he diligently teaches and expounds on the scriptures and various biblical doctrines.

Betty, a Kind, Special, and Weary Woman

April 2012:
Therefore encourage one another and build each other up just as in fact you are doing. (1 Thess. 5:11).

Betty was often late for lunch at the senior care facility where she lived. A kind and pleasant woman, I often needed to remind her when lunch was being served, and she graciously accepted my assistance. It bothered her because she didn't like being late.

One day, I noticed she wasn't in the dining room. I knocked on her door, and she welcomed me into her apartment. She was still wearing her pink robe, sitting on her bed looking tired and upset. I was certain that she wasn't going to make it to the dining room, so I sat with her where she had a box of tissues by her side. Her eyes were red from crying.

Betty had been ill, so very seldom was able to do the activities that she previously liked doing. I was aware of this but didn't know how she felt emotionally about her illness. She began telling me about her physical limitations and how frustrating it was for her because she felt strong mentally. She continued talking while I listened, and my empathy increased as she shared her story. She then said something to me that I will not forget. "I'm just sick of being . . ." There was a pause, and I waited quietly. I knew what she was going to say so I filled in the blank, or the pause and responded. "You're sick of being sick?" She sighed as if relieved and said, "Yes!" Validating her feelings seemed to be medicine for Betty's emotional pain and frustration from being ill. I encouraged her by saying that God is with her and cares for her during this particularly rough time. So often, God uses people in others' lives.

The Holy Spirit acts mysteriously, and that afternoon I was thankful that God used me. I was honored to sit with Betty and listen to her sadness, anxieties, and loss of what she was once physically capable of doing. What I initially thought was a knock on the door to remind her about lunch turned out to be a different kind of help that she needed. She felt emotionally stronger and a few hours later, it dawned on me that God was present in both of our lives. I had a deep sense of peace and joy from being with Betty and listening to her.

God's Infinite Well of Love and Patience

May 16, 2015:
"He gives strength to the weary and increases the power of the weak". (Isa. 40:29).

Working in a rehabilitation center with the elderly is challenging and tiring at times, but it is rewarding. There is nothing like caring for the residents and making a positive difference in their lives. I have learned that in order to care for and about them most effectively, I must rely on God and His love and patience that only He can give. I work twelve-hour shifts and during the last couple of hours, there are times when I run very low on love and patience and find myself becoming weary. I think to myself, I'm finished and can't do this God! Their needs don't stop when my mental, emotional, and physical energy does. It is then I realize that I must solely depend on God and His infinite well of love and patience. So, I ask Him to help me with residents who need special attention and then, something wonderful happens. I walk into the resident's room to discover that I have more tolerance and my energy is restored. It is truly the Lord who gives me His infinite well of love and patience.

Strangers Embracing Forgiveness and Grace

March 29, 2009:

"I will come and proclaim your mighty acts, Sovereign LORD; I will proclaim your righteous deeds, yours alone" (Ps. 71:16).

On March 14, when Steve, and I were vacationing in Florida visiting my mother-in-law Betty, and Steve's aunt and uncle, we had a very serious car accident. We finished having a nice visit and dinner at Uncle Jack and Aunt Pat's home, said goodbye, and got on the road at 11:45 p.m. Within fifteen minutes, Steve said to me, "What is that driver doing? We're going to get hit!" Then before another word could be said, the other driver crashed into our car. He managed to swerve just enough to the left so that a head-on collision was avoided. I was in the front seat and had very minor injuries of one broken bone in my right toe.

The impact of the crash caused my body to shift very close to the dashboard, but the airbag protected me. Steve got minor burns from the air bag and a large bruise on his thigh. Betty, who sat in the back seat, was seriously injured and was air-lifted to a trauma center. She sustained life-threatening injuries that were caused by the impact of the seat belt. She required surgery and with a combination of hospitalization and physical therapy, needed six weeks of treatment.

A few people who witnessed the accident, stopped to help us, and a caring, kind woman gave me her sandals because one of mine got lost. Though Steve and I were in shock, we were able to thank God that we were not seriously injured, but we had no idea what was ahead of us.

Uncle Jack and Aunt Pat drove us to the salvage yard to collect our things from Betty's totaled car. While Steve and I were waiting for assistance, Steve met a man who was standing next to us. They began talking and shortly into the conversation, Steve discovered that this man was the father of the man who crashed into the car. The five of us introduced ourselves to one another, and needless to say, this wasn't an amicable or social conversation. This man, David, was at the salvage yard for the same reason we were, to retrieve any belongings from his son's car. Tyler, David's son, was a college student at a Bible institute and was in a hurry so he wouldn't miss his midnight curfew. He had not been drinking but was speeding at an alarming rate while passing cars on the two lane road. During one of his passes, he was unable to get back in his own lane and hit our car.

The five of us of us began talking and David was very apologetic for the serious accident and the nature of it. Remarkably, he was understanding of the hurt and anger we felt and was kind and polite. Not knowing him, we weren't sure what to think, but at this point we had no reason to believe that he wasn't being genuine. We all walked to the place where the car was and David asked if he could pray with us and for us, and especially for Betty.

Still not knowing what to think about the way this accident and its details were unfolding, Steve and I accepted David's offer of prayer. Even though all of this was surreal, particularly the car accident, God was in full control. I had a peace that can only come from Him. Soon after the crash, David visited Betty every day while in the hospital and when she was in rehabilitation. Steve and I were very grateful for his visits and concern for Betty.

On the last day of our vacation, David invited Steve and I to visit Tyler in the hospital. He shattered his right femur and had surgery to install a replacement rod. Initially, Steve was very apprehensive about meeting the person who caused severe injury to his mother, for he was angry and hurt. All of us were still trying to make sense of this devastating car crash.

I encouraged Steve to go because it was the right thing to do for all of us. Steve changed his mind, and at this point he and David and I had a positive rapport. We walked into Tyler's room. I was using crutches, and Steve followed behind me. Tyler was lying in his bed, looking worn and uncomfortable. I glanced to the right side of the room and saw his mother, Melody. Her eyes were glossy as if she had been crying.

As Tyler began to apologize, I saw a Bible on his right side. He said it would not be right if he didn't ask our forgiveness for causing the accident. I sat down on the edge of his bed, touched his hand, and said, "We forgive you. I don't want you to have that burden. Just get stronger, and better. You have asked our forgiveness, and God hears you." I know the Lord gave the words to me to say in such an uncomfortable, and humanly hopeless situation.

Tyler read a verse from his Bible: "Bear with each other and forgive one another if any of you has a grievance against someone. Forgive as the Lord forgave you" (Col. 3:13). In the middle of reading it, a tear flowed from his eye.

All of the events which had occurred from the moment of the crash to this serious, emotional, and sad moment in Tyler's room, were unbelievable. As I said earlier, God had his hand on this from the moment the accident happened.

After Steve and I returned to Michigan, David called us frequently during Betty's stay in the hospital. He visited her every day and brought her favorite ice cream desert, a Wendy's frosty. David shared his faith in the Lord with Betty, shared the gospel with her, and prayed with her and for her. Their visits were enjoyable. It took Betty several months to fully recover from her injuries, but she did, thank God. Later, David shared with us that he and Tyler drove past the site of the crash and talked about Tyler visiting Betty. Tyler had sent her flowers and a card while she was in the hospital but wanted to meet her in person. I'm sure that visit wasn't easy, but he knew he needed to apologize and take responsibility for causing the accident. David told Steve and I that the visit went well.

I began thinking about that whole incident on a deeper level. A few things came to my mind as I reflected back to that evening. This wasn't about a serious crash, for that sadly happens frequently and isn't extraordinary.

That evening, God allowed the accident to happen, but I wonder if he allowed it so that Steve and I would grow in our faith? What about Tyler and his parents, particularly his father David, who prayed for us upon meeting at the salvage yard that

185

day and never stopped praying for Betty? His care, compassion, and love for her and the Lord were evident.

What about Betty? I focused on the doubt in her faith in God when she expressed earlier that evening about "Not being good enough." I recalled her comments about God and how she wished she were good enough, comparing herself to Billy Graham. The brief conversation with Pat and Jack began when she saw a Billy Graham magazine sitting on the coffee table. As I overheard the conversation, I wanted to tell her that she didn't have to be like Billy Graham. Nobody can ever be good enough, but that God's grace and the gift of salvation is sufficient for anyone who asks for it. Since I wasn't involved in the conversation, I refrained from commenting. I do know this: God is sovereign, and He can and will allow anything to happen.

The accident, the events and people in this story are amazing and mysterious to me, but to God it isn't. "I know that you can do all things, no plan of yours can be thwarted" (Job 42:2). I'm convinced that all of us were strangers, embracing God's grace and forgiveness. His ways are wonderful and perfect. The touch of His hand is too much for me to comprehend. I will praise Him for His great deeds and miracles that He has performed. "Many, LORD my God, are the wonders you have done, the things you planned for us. None can compare with you; were I to speak and tell of your deeds, they would be too many to declare" (Ps. 40:5).

Twelve Years Later

On August 17, 2021 Steve received a call from one of his sisters saying that his mother, Betty, who still lived in Florida, was in the hospital due to complications from congestive heart failure. The medical staff recommended that the family visit for she may be nearing the end of her life. Upon getting this news, I contacted Melody, David's wife, and said to her, "I wanted to tell you that Betty is in the hospital having serious problems with her congestive heart failure, and not doing well. Please pray for her. My biggest prayer is that she knows Jesus Christ as her Savior. I know David has had many talks with her and had prayed for her and with her after the accident. I know you have too! Thank you."

Melody responded: "I'm sorry to hear that, Robin! Thank you for letting us know! Can you let us know which hospital she is in and whether they allow visitors, and maybe David can visit her?"

Shortly after Melody's first message, I got this message: "Hi Robin, David visited Betty on Wednesday evening, and they had a lovely visit. Betty expressed again that she was frightened about dying, so he asked her if she were certain where she would go when she died? She was not, so he reviewed the plan of salvation emphasizing God's grace and the need to trust in His Son Jesus Christ. He prayed a prayer of salvation with her, and David said she had peace afterward, and she seemed comforted. I just wanted you to know because I know you have been concerned for her. We appreciate you keeping us posted! God bless"!

We lost Betty September 13, 2021. Shortly after that, Steve called David to tell him. Steve and I were very thankful for the conversation we had with David. During that memorable and very important visit with David, Betty indeed believed and received the Lord as her Savior. David went into further detail about his visit with her as he explained to Betty about God's grace and forgiveness of sins. David, Melody, Steve and

I are thankful and have joy and peace for those moments that David spent with her. It's a miracle! As we marveled at God's amazing grace, we ended the conversation by David quoting a Bible verse. "The Lord is not slow in keeping his promise, as some understand slowness. Instead he is patient with you, not wanting anyone to perish, but everyone to come to repentance". (2 Pet. 3:9).

Faithful Workouts

2018:

In 2014, I began exercising to an online workout called "Faithful Workouts." Michelle, founder, fitness expert and trainer offers over two hundred workouts of various levels that consists of many different cross training exercises. I was so glad to have found this program because she had everything I needed to stay fit. With a strong emphasis on biblical principles, she teaches if you're healthy, strong, and physically fit, then you'll be more equipped to serve God and love others. I have personally found this to be true in my life, and I am so grateful to exercise with someone who is very positive, energetic and uplifting through her exercise ministry.

In February 2018, I joined Faithful Workouts Facebook group page, and decided to post. It had been snowing all day, accumulating twelve inches! As I was working on my manuscript, I looked out the window at our beautiful snow-covered backyard. On my post, I mentioned being thankful for the blueberry jam, peanut butter, and other sweet treasures that I had gotten from Katie for Christmas. I also said that I was eagerly awaiting my Faithful Workouts t-shirt that I ordered from their store. I concluded my post by commenting on the lovely snowfall.

A Treasured and Unique Friendship

"Each of you should give what you have decided in your heart to give, not reluctantly or under compulsion, for God loves a cheerful giver" (2 Cor. 9:7).

In everything I did, I showed you that by this kind of hard work we must help the weak, remembering the words the Lord Jesus himself said: "It is more blessed to give than to receive". (Acts 20:35)

Christine, who then worked administratively for Faithful Workouts, commented on my post. She liked my thoughts and noticed how I appreciated each moment of the day. Soon after, we started chatting via social media.

In April 2019, I earnestly prayed to see if it was appropriate and in the will of God, to send Christine the introduction of my manuscript. She read it and appreciated the beginning of my story. She said she understood depression and anxiety for she had experienced it after losing her mother and grandmother within four months of each other. Our friendship continued and eventually we began chatting on the phone.

Christine is an artist and published author who has written three devotions that are featured in a magazine called *Faith on Every Corner*. She has a shop called Living Word Décor. She designs and creates all of her items. They are lovely, and she uses her God-given talents to create a variety of products that are scripturally based. She is a faithful and loyal servant of Jesus

Christ, who has great compassion and love for others. We have become prayer warriors for one another. She prays for me and my friends, my family, and my residents at work, all of whom she has never personally met. I pray for her, her family, her animals, and her art business.

In May 2021, she sent one of her art pieces to one of my residents, Celia, who enjoys art and is artistic and creative. Christine asked me what her favorite Bible verse and color was, so one evening I asked Celia those questions. She told me that purple was her favorite color, and she had several favorite Bible verses. So I peeked in her Bible and saw a couple of verses from Psalm 139 she had written in her notes. Christine made a white wooden rectangular sign with purple flowers and green leaves on two corners. In the center, she creatively wrote Psalm 139:13–14: "For you created my inmost being, you knit me together in my mother's womb. I praise you because I am fearfully and wonderfully made." She also gave her an adult coloring book with many lovely pictures and Bible verses, and a small box of cards with different words that describe God.

I thank God for Christine and her acts of love and kindness. She made an incredible impact on someone who, like many elderly folks, suffered in so many ways during the Covid-19 pandemic. Celia could not have smiled bigger the day I gave those gifts to her. Christine genuinely loves Celia and has a special compassion for the elderly.

CHAPTER 40

My Much-Loved Siblings, Nieces, and Nephews

Y sister and brother share an important and special role in my life. As the youngest sibling, I'll always be Robbie to Jimmy, my brother, and I love hearing that. Nobody else calls me that. When Janice calls me and needs to leave a voicemail she still says, "This is your big sister," and it doesn't matter what the life situation is, she's always had my back and always will. She consistently demonstrates a tough love and compassion. As I wrote earlier, my sister and brother were always supportive and loving during adolescence when I had the onset of bipolar disorder. I especially found this to be evident during the dark season of deep depression. I value the sense of humor that we all have, which I believe mostly comes from our mother, for she had a natural wit and sarcasm. We are close and while together have special moments that draw us closer as the years pass.

Jenny and Jimmy, as parents to Zack, I admire your deep care and love for him. Your involved parenting has produced a high achieving son. You have been so supportive in every area of his life. Jenny, your appreciation for the institution of marriage and the family is greatly admired and clearly evident with your family and our family.

Mark, you are more like a brother to me than a brother-in-law. You manage to know all of our family stories and thoroughly enjoy making fun of them! I'll never forget the first time I met you on one of your early dates with Janice when you came to the house. I was fourteen and impulsively said some pretty silly and crazy things which embarrassed Janice, and she wanted to kill me, but you came back! I love laughing with you, and in spite of Janice telling me, "Don't laugh it just encourages him," I can't help it; you're funny! You are a family man which I appreciate, and you've seen the fruits of that with Kelli and Dan, and now you're enjoying your much-loved granddaughters, Cece and Elliot.

Kelli, my sweet niece, you're all grown up and now you're married and a mother of two precious daughters. I'm so proud of you. You love and care for your husband, Aaron and children, Cece and Elliot with all of your heart. A cute and funny memory of you is when you were about four years old, and I gave you a piece of Bubble Yum. It was too big for you and the sugary juice from the gum just dripped out of your mouth. No, I didn't tell your mother! You are ambitious and work so diligently in everything you do. Our family and your friends know that you are very funny, possessing a great sense of humor which you get so honestly! On a serious note, from the day I told you I wanted to publish my writings and sent the introduction to you, you took such an interest and passion in it. Your encouragement and and technical support with my writings and book layout is so appreciated.

Aaron, I'm so happy that Kelli has you as a loving husband and very attentive father to Cece and Elliot. I first learned of your calm and patient nature when Cece, who was not quite two years old, had a little meltdown and was pitifully crying. You simply smiled as if you knew it wouldn't last. Your personality, I'm sure, will come in handy when Cece and Elliot are teenagers! Your musical and artistic talents that God has given to you are impressive, and I know Kelli appreciates them. Cece and Elliot have fun as you play the guitar or make art projects with them.

Dan, I can still see you playing with Michael and Katie in Grandma and Grandpa's backyard. It wasn't a spacious one, but the three of you managed to play ball with that little yellow plastic bat and whiffle ball. You are a faithful and loyal person and a fine nephew. I see you demonstrate these traits with your parents, sister and two little nieces. I appreciate your kindness to me, and smile when I send you a message or call because I know I'm going to receive a quick response. When I sent a few excerpts from my book, you read it and took time to comment on it. A special thanks to you.

Zack, the earliest memory I have of you is you running around Grandma and Grandpa Lewis's home with such high energy, playing with your older cousins, Michael and Katie. You just couldn't sit still. You were so cute and entertaining! God has given you athletic ability that your parents saw as early as age three years old. Seeing you at the tennis nationals when you were seventeen was so much fun, and we were so proud of you. Now, you're in medical school studying diligently to be a doctor. Soon you will reap the benefits of your persistence and endless determination to become one. I noticed when you were in college that you were kind, caring, and sensitive to other's needs. You will be a fine doctor. How thoughtful of you to read the introduction of my book, considering how busy you were with your medical studies.

Cece, you are my pleasant and lively four-year-old great niece who has a lot to say for such a little girl. You are a lot of fun, and I really enjoy being with you as you share what's happening in your world. You definitely have an enthusiasm for life, which I appreciate. I like running around with you at your Grandma and Grandpa's home when we play hide and seek. It's also fun playing with your Barbies and your other toys. I especially enjoy when you run to me from across the room, and we give each other a hug.

Elliot, you're my high spirited two-year-old great niece who seems to not have any troubles letting your parents, your big sister, or any of your family know what you need or want in your world. I like your determination! A particular memory I have of you is when you were thirteen months old, and I was riding on your little train with you, and I accidentally ran over your foot. We had a rough start! Later, when Uncle Steve and I visited you shortly before your second birthday, we had a really fun time. I pulled those colorful and shiny beads out of my bag and you got really excited. You chose the one you liked and wore it the rest of the day. Later, you gave me a hug, which I loved. Your parents told me that you really like sunglasses, and I've seen cute pictures of you wearing them. You look so cute and stylish! I understand you don't like taking them off once you get a pair that you really like. Enjoy your sunglasses Elliot, when you're on the beach or anywhere you go, even if you're indoors!

CeCe and Elliot, I gave each of you a special gift after you were born. I printed several Bible verses from Psalm 139 onto card stock paper and placed the paper in a picture frame.

Always know that I love you, and you are very special to me, but in God's eyes you are uniquely wonderful and deeply loved.

> For you created my inmost being; you knit me together in my mother's womb. I praise you because I am fearfully and wonderfully made; your works are wonderful, I know that full well. My frame was not hidden from you when I was made in the secret place, when I was woven together in the depths of the earth. Your eyes saw my unformed body; all the days ordained for me were written in your book before one of them came to be. (Ps. 139:13–16).

Living with Bipolar Today

*I*n the early eighties, I wrote in my journal that I thought I was free from bipolar disorder. I sincerely thought after I stopped taking the medication that God had healed me. Through the years of experiencing mood swing episodes, I have discovered that I will always have this mood disorder until the day I make my home in heaven. What causes bipolar disorder? As a teenager, I certainly didn't know or fully comprehend why I had it.

> The exact cause of bipolar disorder is unknown, but several factors may be involved, such as:
> Biological differences. People with bipolar disorder appear to have physical changes in their brains. The significance of these changes is still uncertain but may eventually help pinpoint causes.
> Genetics. Bipolar disorder is more common in people who have a first-degree relative, such as a sibling or parent, with the condition. Researchers are trying to find genes that may be involved in causing bipolar disorder.
> "Bipolar Disorder-Symptoms, and Causes", Mayo Clinic, February 16, 2021

The genetic factor relates to me. My mother struggled with depression at different times in her life, but I actually didn't realize that until I was in my early thirties. Even then, I didn't fully understand the genetic component until I delved into writing my book. She didn't experience the symptoms of mania like I did, but I do remember many times while growing up she was very happy and so often made me laugh hysterically, for she had a quick-witted sense of humor. At the same time, there were many years that she struggled with sadness and depression, often suffering from insomnia which exacerbated the depression. It saddens me that she experienced sadness and despair at different times of her life. She was so instrumental in getting the professional help for me but, ironically, didn't get help for herself.

Both of my parents cared deeply about my struggle with bipolar disorder, but my mother, particularly, offered great wisdom to me about the illness. She taught me that I should liken it to diabetes or heart disease with a special emphasis on taking care of my body. While heart disease and diabetes are not mental illnesses, they are health conditions that require proper medical attention. I learned that these diseases could cause depression and that physical illnesses can affect people mentally. This advice was instilled in me and also helped me to not feel crazy during adolescence when the body is experiencing hormonal changes.

Back in 2012, I told one of my managers at work that I had bipolar disorder. The only reason I shared that with her was to tell her about God and glorify Him. Recently I shared with someone that I had bipolar disorder, and her response was: "You have it all together!" My doctor in 2017 said, "I've never met anyone like you who only takes one medication. Most people take two or three of them." I know I am very fortunate and beyond blessed by God to have only taken one medication, lithium. Lithium, as my doctor told me, is a charm if it works. For some people, it doesn't work, but it did for me and was the perfect medication. It brought me out of the initial onset of the illness back in 1977 and four years later, when I was a senior in high school, it worked for me again. My situation is unique, and why is this? Besides my parents teaching me the importance of taking my medicine, there are other significant reasons that I "have it all together" and have only taken one medicine.

In high school, there were several times I was asked to smoke marijuana and drink alcohol, but I refused. During adolescence and the college years, God protected me from illegal drugs and alcohol. My doctor said to me when I was in my late teens to not take a drug like PCP(Commonly known as "Angel Dust"). I didn't understand why he said that, but it had to do with my brain chemistry. I learned that taking mood-altering drugs are even more detrimental to someone who has a mental health condition like bipolar disorder. If I had taken this drug, it could have sent me into a whirlwind of high mood swings, and I may have believed that I could jump off a cliff or the Empire State Building!

Going back to her comment, "You have it all together", my answer was absolutely not! It was not me. I said that having a relationship with Jesus Christ was what enabled me to have my life together. My friend who asked me that question suffered from bipolar disorder. God knew that one day I would tell a friend my account, my journey, and His miraculous work in my life. It's because of His Son Jesus Christ that I am truly able to appreciate every season of my life.

"You make known to me the path of life; you will fill me with your joy in your presence, with eternal pleasures at your right hand" (Ps. 16:11).

February through May 2021, when I experienced that unexpected stretch of depression, I was once again reminded that I will always have bipolar disorder and periodically struggle with moments of mania and depression. That's perfectly fine with me! I've really never known any other way since I was fourteen years old. Some day after I leave this world and enter into the presence of my Savior, I will no longer have a mood disorder that God allowed.

> For you created my inmost being; you knit me together in my mother's womb. I praise you because I am fearfully and wonderfully made; your works are wonderful, I know that full well. My frame was not hidden from you when I was made in the secret place, when I was woven together in the depths of the earth. Your eyes saw my unformed body; all the days ordained for me were written in your book before one of them came to be. (Ps. 139:13–16).

Until my life on this earth ends, I will share with others the joy and love I have because of the Lord's love for me.

I will sing to the Lord all my life; I will sing praise to my God as long as I live (Ps. 104:33).

Bibliography

Bailey, Kasee. "Five Powerful Health Benefits of Journaling." Intermountain Healthcare. Last accessed July 31, 2018, https://intermountainhealthcare.org/blogs/topics/live-well/2018/07/5-powerful-health-bene-fits-of-journaling.

Balzer, Deb Mayo Clinic Minute: "Is a Rise in Teen Depression Linked to Technology, Social media?" Accessed April 1, 2019, Https://www.bing.com/search/q=mayoclinicminutes+a+rise+in+depres-sion+by+deb+balzer&cvid=f772a.

Keveran, Phillip Chorus, and Orchestra, "A Quiet Place." In Pastures Green, Ralph Carmichael. Discovery House Music, Grand Rapids, Michigan 2013, CD.

Keveran, Phillip Chorus and Orchestra, "Timeless One." In Pastures Green, Phillip Keveran. Discovery House Music, Grand Rapids, Michigan 2013, CD.

Gokey, Danny, "Tell Your Heart to Beat Again." Hope In Front of Me," Bernie Herms, Randy Phillips, Matthew West. BMG Rights Management, New York, New York, 2014, CD.

Mayo Clinic, Bipolar Disorder-Symptoms, and Causes. Patient Care & Health information, Diseases and

Conditions. Accessed February 16, 2021, https://www/ mayo clinic.org/diseases-conditions/bipolar-disorder/ symptoms/causes/syc-20355.

Saffles, Gretchen "Five Reasons to Journal Daily", "An Article by Gretchen Saffles", Accessed March 11, 2021, https:// Well Watered Women.com/five-reasons-to-journal-daily.

Tomlin, Chris, "Waterfall," "Love Ran Red" Chris Tomlin, Sixstepsrecords, Roswell, Georgia, 2014, CD.

.

CPSIA information can be obtained
at www.ICGtesting.com
Printed in the USA
BVHW070053010223
657531BV00007B/215

9 781662 860430